SOWING SEEDS OF WONDER

SOWING SEEDS
OF WONDER

*The Stories of Ruth and Charles Larabee
and the Origins of San Diego Botanic Garden*

Sally Sandler

Second, Expanded Edition
Printed by CreateSpace
An Amazon.com Company

ISBN-10: 1-5301-7720-0
ISBN-13: 978-1-5301-7720-2
Printed by CreateSpace, An Amazon.com Company
Available from Amazon.com, CreateSpace.com,
and other retail outlets.

Cover photograph: Rachel Cobb

DEDICATION

To the staff and volunteers at San Diego Botanic Garden,
and to all who visit this magical place.

CONTENTS

FOREWORD

At long last we have the true story of the Larabees and the beginning of what we now know of as San Diego Botanic Garden. There have been many stories passed on by word of mouth about Ruth and Charles Larabee, and now we can discard those which were not true.

When I first arrived in 1995 as the Executive Director of what was then called Quail Botanical Gardens, I found myself, like so many others, extremely interested in understanding what we knew about the Larabees, since they clearly were important in establishing this public garden. One of the stories I was told is that Ruth Larabee was a widow when she deeded the property to San Diego County in the mid-1950s. Furthermore, I was told that Charles was tragically lost at sea and that neither he nor his boat was ever recovered from a time when he sailed out on his own.

This of course was not true, and the genuine story of the Larabees is far more interesting in its factual telling than in any of the fiction that preceded it.

Sally Sandler has done the extensive detective work we needed to put together this remarkable true story. She is an excellent example of the Gardens' many very talented volunteers and docents. And as you will read and enjoy, Sally proved expertly suited for this task.

San Diego Botanic Garden will forever be indebted to Sally for the countless hours she contributed by interviewing individuals who knew the Larabees and by researching documents located far and wide. Her research work and talent for relating her findings has resulted in the fascinating opportunity we now have to really know these unique people.

While neither Ruth nor Charles could likely have envisioned what their home and land would become, the two children's gardens that make up a very important part of the visitor experience at San Diego Botanic Garden today share a particularly profound connection with the Larabee heritage.

You see, while the Larabees did not have children of their own, during the 1940s and 50s they spent a great deal of their time and energy connecting young people to the wonder and beauty of the outdoors. Both of them had a strong affinity for nature and realized that exposing children to nature and inspiring them about it was important in their development.

In our present day environment, when children have so much electronic entertainment to occupy themselves with indoors, what the Larabees saw as important decades ago has become an epidemic of need. So watching children enjoying the outdoors and having their imaginations stimulated by being at San Diego Botanic Garden would certainly make both Ruth and Charles smile.

—JULIAN DUVAL
PRESIDENT/CEO, SAN DIEGO BOTANIC GARDEN
ENCINITAS, CALIFORNIA
2016

ACKNOWLEDGEMENTS

I am grateful to the following organizations and individuals who readily supplied me with help and resources: The Archives and Special Collections at Vassar College Libraries, the Barstow School, the Development Office of Texas Tech University, the Encinitas Historical Society, Mark Massen and the San Diego County Parks and Recreation Department, Nicholas Paoni, photographer, the Nora E. Larabee Memorial Library of Stafford, Kansas, the San Diego County Office of Records, the San Diego History Center, the San Diego Natural History Museum, the San Dieguito Heritage Museum, and the University of California-Santa Barbara Library Aerial Imagery Research Service, Map and Imagery Lab.

To all the former Scouts we interviewed—Jan (Waite) Bittner, Richard Cullum, Carol (Hasselo) French, Doug Hasselo, Connie (Conrad) Lund, Janet McNulty, Miki Nagata, Marcie Phillips, and Bob Gooding—and to Gerald Cullison, Caroline Isaacs, William Hopkins, Jr., Debra Judson Earle, Esther Newman, Jean Schneider, and Nelani Midgley Walker— thanks for your wonderful memories.

I've been extraordinarily fortunate to have three of the best possible editors: My husband, Jim Sandler; my sister Ellen

LaConte, an accomplished fiction and non-fiction author; and Dave Ehrlinger, the former Director of Horticulture, who has been a joy to collaborate with thanks to his extensive knowledge of the Garden and his fondness for history.

To each and every one of the following people, I am deeply indebted for your generous support, encouragement, and advice: Julian Duval, Steve Brigham, Rachel Cobb, Robbie Elliott, Stacy Fattaleh, Pat Hammer, Kenneth Hayward, Joe Libertini, Karen May, Heidrun Meador, Barbara Osthaus, Susan Starr, the late Bill Teague, Susan Wegner, Lucy Chase Williams and Bart Williams, the docents and volunteers of San Diego Botanic Garden, and Lynda Whan, who in 2006 suggested I return to a place called Quail Botanical Gardens.

PREFACE

Unlike many other movers and shakers in San Diego's history, Ruth and Charles Larabee have the distinction of being largely unknown. Even in San Diego's North County where the celebrated 37-acre botanic garden they initiated in the 1940s and 50s is located, few know who they were. Their surname sounds vaguely western, like Fort Laramie, Wyoming, hinting at cowboys and the Wild West (which in Charles' case does have some validity), like something familiar you should be able to but can't quite place.

The modest ranch home that the Larabees occupied stands in the middle of San Diego Botanic Garden with their name painted on a rustic wooden sign. They are mentioned on the Garden's website, and a handful of photos picturing them can be found in what was once their living room. They still exist in the memories of the few aging Explorer and Girl Scouts and Camp Fire Girls who knew them way back when. But beyond that, little is known and even less understood about the Larabees.

Perhaps our relative unfamiliarity with the Larabees is in part because Ruth and Charles were difficult to label. They were a complex, unconventional couple who didn't match any stereotype of their time and didn't fit neatly into any one mold. They were both educated and privileged during a period when much of the country was experiencing the hardships of the Great Depression. They did not seem to be bound by tradition. They were adventurers and collectors and travelled extensively when World War II gripped most of the world and nations focused on survival and wartime industry.

In later years, their lives diverged dramatically, so they couldn't be spoken of easily as a unit. They had no children with whom to share their story and who could later interpret it for us. There were a very limited number of records preserved in photos and letters. Their names don't appear in the annals with other San Diego founders, though in time they may rightfully stand alongside those formidable peers. Were they ranchers, gardeners, youth leaders? What they were is difficult to pin down.

That difficulty is what gave rise to this book. Sometime in spring 2010 while tending some of the beds in the Walled Garden outside the Larabees' former house I was approached by a visitor with questions about the founders of Quail Botanical Gardens (now called San Diego Botanic Garden.) Who were these people, she wanted to know, and were they independently wealthy or did they have to work for a living while also running the ranch?

Even though for years we had been concentrating on developing the garden surrounding their home, we were completely unprepared for questions about who had actually lived inside it. Nothing in the docent training manuals provided the answers, so the solution was to go to the top, to the office of Julian Duval, President and CEO of San Diego Botanic Garden. In conversations about Ruth and Charles and their history, Duval alluded to the handful of rumors and legends that had been circulating for years. But overall, there was still a tremendous void where the history of our Garden's founders should exist.

One year and 400 pages of documents later, we finally had some answers to the visitor's question and the mystery of the Larabees. A few of those early rumors were confirmed, but for the most part the Larabees' story was far more complex and remarkable than we might have guessed.

Ruth and Charles Larabee, with their unconventional personal lives and complex backgrounds, were civic-minded individuals who made a significant contribution to generations of people seeking a connection to nature.

The Larabees took a bold risk by acquiring a rustic ranch in Southern California with the idea of transforming it into someplace extraordinary. They were passionate about finding and planting rare and unusual species that flourished in San Diego's Mediterranean climate. They shared natural wonders and the outdoors with eager young people, sowing the seeds for future generations of nature lovers.

Ruth Larabee practiced wildlife conservation about 20 years ahead of the Endangered Species Act and the national environmental protections that came with it. And ultimately she was the visionary who gave her land to San Diego County to preserve its rare natural habitat and endangered species and inspire botanical wonder in people of all ages.

Today, the botanic garden where the Larabees sowed the seeds is visited by thousands of people from around the world each year. It is a garden oasis amidst a sprawling city, an urban retreat with four miles of scenic trails that provides a peaceful setting for the public to experience nature's beauty. It is a wildlife sanctuary that strives to educate the public about plants and their vital role in human lives and the natural environment.

San Diego Botanic Garden, where the Larabees established 200 different plant species, has grown to a collection of 19 geographic and themed gardens woven together by lush landscapes and a collection of over 4,000 different species today. Each year it is host to countless weddings, anniversaries, celebrations and other large events. Goals of the Garden incorporate conservation, plant introduction, cultivation, and evaluation, and historic preservation, while inspiring people of all ages to connect with plants and nature.

Distinctive features include world class collections of bamboo, aloes, agaves, palms and cycads, outstanding children's gardens, and coveys of quail that Ruth adored. The Garden is still growing, poised to expand with an education conservatory in the near future. It's doubtful the Larabees could possibly have imagined how the seed they planted would grow and how many people's lives would be enriched by their generous gift.

Now we have the opportunity to learn more about this unique couple, and in so doing to honor their legacy going forward.

—SALLY SANDLER

SAN DIEGO, CALIFORNIA

2016

SINCE THE ORIGINAL publication of this book in 2016, members of Ruth Baird Larabee's extended family contacted us at San Diego Botanic Garden. Lucy Chase Williams and her brother Marcus (Bart) Williams, Ruth's great-niece and nephew, have a trove of letters and photos from their Aunt Ruth's early years which they shared during their memorable visit. Ruth's story was so expanded and enriched by these personal expressions that a second edition of this book was called for. We are profoundly grateful for their warmth, friendship and contributions.

—SALLY SANDLER
SAN DIEGO, CALIFORNIA
2017

I will try to give a page of my life which would lie near the front of my biography did such a valuable work exist. A gulf of time separates that day from this. Apropos of gulf, all my life seems to be connected with water ... and although I know that in some respects I am not different from other children, yet water does seem peculiarly my element. In the first place, I am unnaturally fond of soda water. Then I am better able to swim than to walk. I have always been fond of walking through puddles, too. I feel quite sure I shall come to a watery grave.

Ruth Baird Robertson (Ruth Larabee) age 16, in 1920
Kansas City, Kansas

The greatest satisfaction in my disordered life has come from my contact with Nature.

Ruth Baird Larabee, age 56, in 1960
Puebla, Mexico

CHAPTER I

AUSPICIOUS BEGINNINGS

Every book is a quotation; and every house is a quotation
out of all forests, and mines, and stone quarries;
and every man is a quotation from all his ancestors.

—RALPH WALDO EMERSON

From the day she was born in 1904, the stars seemed to be aligned in Ruth Larabee's favor. Christened Ruth Robertson Baird, she was the first born of a pair of intellectuals living in the stimulating academic environment of the University of Michigan in Ann Arbor. Her parents both graduated from Michigan with bright futures and the promise of success ahead. It was near the end of the Gilded Age when industrialization promised rewards and opportunity for all Americans, and hopes for the future were still high.

Ruth Baird was a product of fifth generation Americans whose lineage was English/Scotch-Irish. Her Baird ancestors followed the footsteps of those who escaped the Irish potato famine in the 1840s and '50s seeking refuge and paid work in the churning factories of America's East Coast cities.

As a school girl, Ruth was no stranger to wealth and the comfortable, protected lifestyle it conferred. Her family lived in one of the finest homes in Kansas City, a three-acre estate with forest trees on Sunset Drive overlooking a country club, and their household included a nurse and an African American cook. It's easy to imagine that her childhood was occupied with climbing trees, wading in streams, gazing in wonder at butterflies and other things one might find in a wooded back yard. In addition, as the first born child she was probably the focus of much adult attention and most likely grew up eager to meet her parents' high expectations.

RUTH'S PARENTS CHARLES A. Baird and Georgia Oriana Robertson met while they were each students at the University of Michigan during a time when a college education was usually reserved for people of privilege who were also predominantly white and male. In fact, near the turn of the century when Georgia graduated, only 19 percent of college or university degrees were awarded to women.[1]

Born in Vanceburg, Kentucky, Charles Baird enrolled at the University of Michigan in 1890 as a student in the literature department. He wore the Michigan Wolverines maize and blue jersey as a football player beginning in 1891 and was elected to the athletic board as its freshman representative. In 1893, he was designated the manager of the football team and held that position for three seasons.

After receiving his Bachelor's Degree in literature in 1895, Baird was employed as the football team's manager, reportedly "by reason of his business ability."[2] In 1898 the finances of the Michigan Athletic Association were at low ebb, so the University looked to him to make improvements as Michigan's first Director of Athletics, a position he retained until 1909.[3]

Charles and Georgia were married in Ann Arbor in 1902.[4] She was the daughter of John Duffy Robertson, president of Kansas City's Interstate National Bank. Ruth was born in Ann Arbor two years later on February 28, 1904. A year after his father-in-law died in 1908, Charles moved Georgia and Ruth and his father Lyman Baird to Kansas City so he could anchor the bank Georgia's father left behind. Not long after, the Bairds had two more children, Mary Eloise and James Robert.

Gerald Cullison, the Assistant Superintendent of Park Operation and Maintenance for San Diego County, recalled what Ruth told him about their move from Michigan to Kansas in 1909. "She was still a small child when ... they moved west. For reasons unknown, they did this in a covered wagon," Cullison said. "Space was so limited they had to dispose of all their furniture, but Ruth's grandfather insisted on keeping the grandfather clock. She said the children figured out later why that piece was so important. The clock was where their grandfather hid his whiskey."[5]

Moving in a covered wagon seems improbable given images we've come to associate with it, like wagon trains, riflemen and the lumbering Conestoga "schooners" of the past. However, bicycles, carriages and wagons of all types still rolled people over thousands of miles of roads in the early 1900s.[6]

Eventually Baird became engaged in the investment and farm mortgage business, purchased the Western Exchange Bank in Kansas City and was elected president. At various times he was also a director of the Inter-State National Bank, a director of the Morris Plan Company, and treasurer of the Anchor Savings and Loan Association, all in Kansas City.[7] Baird was praised as "a capitalist of Kansas City" at a time when that was a high honor. In 1911 he entered into negotiations to purchase the Boston National League baseball team but ultimately decided against it. During that prosperous period in their lives, Charles and Georgia invested heavily in property in Texas and various Midwestern states around Kansas.

Unfortunately, Georgia died from complications of a heart condition at age 47 in 1923, during Ruth's sophomore year at Vassar. Charles shouldered the responsibility of raising all three children until sometime after 1930 when he married a woman named Katherine Adams, also a University of Michigan alumna. In his later years together with Katherine, Baird became a benefactor of the University of Michigan and a widely noted philanthropist. He and Katherine remained in Kansas City until he died of a heart attack in 1944. He was buried in the family plot in Kansas City next to Ruth's mother Georgia.

FOR STUDENTS AND alumni of the University of Michigan, the name Baird literally rings a bell. The Charles Baird Carillon, a central campus landmark and the third heaviest carillon in the world, is housed in the Burton Memorial Tower. It has marked every quarter hour faithfully for eight decades of students, visitors, professors and dignitaries. The carillon was purchased in 1936 with a $70,000 gift from Charles Baird.[8] Not only did Ruth and her siblings have in their father a model of business acumen and financial success, but also an excellent exemplar of generosity.

Indeed, high achieving, philanthropic men were prevalent in Ruth's heritage. Her uncle James Baird also played Wolverine football and graduated from the University of Michigan to become a successful civil engineer. He directed the construction of many significant American landmarks, including the Flatiron Building in New York City, the Lincoln Memorial, the Arlington Memorial Amphitheater and Tomb of the Unknown Soldier in Washington, D.C., and the Law School at his alma mater, the University of Michigan in Ann Arbor.[9]

Later the younger Baird brother gave 590 acres of farmland to the state of New York with the stipulation that it be established as the James Baird State Park. Today the park includes a renowned golf course, spacious open and wooded picnic areas, seven miles of hiking trails and a sports complex. Donating valuable land and philanthropy in general were recurring themes in the Baird family dynasty.[10]

NOT ONLY WAS Ruth Baird well provided for, but like her parents, she was also well educated, attending prestigious private schools in her post-elementary years.

In 1917 she began studies at The Barstow School, a private, coed K-12 prep school in Kansas City. As a member of the Class of 1922, Ruth was active on *The Weather-cock* yearbook staff as a contributing writer. The staff page of the *The Weather-cock* lists Ruth among the editors of the enticingly named "Scandalous Club," which may have been the literary portion of the publication. She also participated in a theater club called "The Pretenders" and balanced her extracurricular activities by playing on the high school women's basketball team and being active in Camp Fire Girls.

Young Ruth's character can be glimpsed through portions of her wartime story featured in the 1919 *Weather-cock*, entitled "When Freddie Came Marching Home":

Mrs. Fred Stanton, Sr., smiled with perfect happiness as she folded the dispatch in her usual careful way. For had she not just received news of her boy's long expected arrival in New York, and was he not even now speeding toward her? Yes, she would see Fred Saturday night. Then she frowned as she remembered the last phrase in the telegram: "Hope to see Marion."

Now, Mrs. Stanton was an absolutely honest woman but also she was a fond mother and when her son had written wistfully of the other fellows' letters from girls at home, she had almost regretted that they had lived nearly entirely in England, so that Fred's young friends were few.

Therefore, when new neighbors had moved in next door, she had written minutely of the daughter, Marion Daniel, who "looked like the princess in the fairy tale." Fred had seemed so interested that she had even dared to write him that Miss Daniel would not mind if he enclosed a letter to her. This he had done, writing more promptly than usual, and she had answered in the person of Miss Daniel.

It had now been six months, however, since she had started her deception ... so she had made a brave resolution ... By Saturday she would have interested Miss Daniel to such an extent that the latter would be willing to take the actual place of Fred's correspondent. Miss Daniel was excited, and seemed really anxious to be a party to this most disgraceful proceeding.

Saturday evening our hero stepped off the train and gazed with eagerness into the mob about him. He found his mother, grabbed her, and then stood waiting with shy expectancy to see the girl he knew through their correspondence. Then he met what is indeed unusual in this weary world, a dream come true! And the mother seeing the light in his eyes found her happiness in theirs."[11]

What a captivating story from the young ninth-grader. Consistent with her age and the era, Ruth was an incorrigible romantic, empathizing with a mother's desperate hopes for her war hero son, searching for something uplifting to do for him during the violent destruction of WWI, and scheming a bit to make it all happen.

Ruth also had considerable faith in what a devoted mother might well do. The story was the product of an active imagination written by someone comfortable with a pen and familiar with the requirements of a well-crafted story.

A year later, Ruth took up the pen once more, this time composing the lively and humorous "My Element" for her 1920 yearbook, portions of which follow:

I will try to give a page of my life which would lie near the front of my biography did such a valuable work exist. A gulf of time separates that day from this. Apropos of gulf, all my life seems to be connected with water—this especial episode itself merely a little island in my history—and although I know that in some respects I am not different from other children yet water does seem peculiarly my element. In the first place I

7

am unnaturally fond of soda water: then I am better able to swim than to walk. I have always been fond of walking through puddles, too—I feel quite sure I shall come to a watery grave.

One morning … my friend Rachel and I were busy washing our doll dishes at the rain barrel which stood at the back of her house. We were standing on a high bench scrabbling earnestly at the cups which had contained chocolate in the form of mud and at the big platter, our treasure, which had held a huge turkey of the same substance.

After seeing Rachel scrub and scrub vainly in her effort to cleanse the platter I wrenched it from her and scraped so hard that even the pink roses on it disappeared, then I suddenly dropped the object of my zeal and it sank clear to the bottom of the barrel.

I dripped or rather flowed on and very considerately went in the kitchen door when a worse calamity assailed me, for the cook had just scrubbed the floor, and some of the slippery suds adhered to it still so that when my feet touched the floor they immediately left it to fly out behind me, projecting my face and flying hair into a fly paper which the cook had left on the floor."[12]

This playful story illustrates Ruth Baird's appreciation for sarcasm and even a little mischief. Her theatrical background is evident when she describes scenes which would be slapstick if performed on the stage. The privileged lifestyle she most likely took for granted is apparent in her reference to the cook who had just scrubbed the floor.

On a more ominous note, however, when viewed later from the end of Ruth's life, this premonition of "a watery grave," or death at the hands of the elements represents an eerie foreshadowing of what the future would hold in store for the young writer.

The teenaged Ruth was not a classic beauty, but neither was she plain. Dressed in a blouse with sailor collar and tie and frowning into the sun, she stood out from the crowd of fellow female students by virtue of the openness of her broad face, full lips, long dark hair pulled into a pony tail and a certain directness that lent a classic composure to her appearance.

Ruth was an avid reader in high school, and family members recall her intense interest in the biography of Abraham Lincoln.

During her years at Barstow, Ruth became one of the earliest members of the Camp Fire Girls organization. Sometime around 1918 when she was 14 years old, she earned the high rank of Torch Bearer and personally hand crafted the Native American-inspired ceremonial costume, complete with a beaded, full-length gown and handmade moccasins which were typical of that achievement.

In her junior and senior years, Ruth attended the prestigious Emma Willard School, a boarding school for high school students, in Troy, New York, from which she graduated in 1922.

DURING RUTH BAIRD'S school years the times had been changing in America, especially for young women. For example, the

Nineteenth Amendment guaranteeing all adult American women the right to vote was ratified by Congress in 1920. After graduation, Ruth decided to study Latin at Vassar College in Poughkeepsie, New York, placing herself at the leading edge of the growing numbers of American women in higher education. When she graduated with a Bachelor's Degree in 1926, the number of women college graduates had risen to 39 percent.[13]

Ruth's graduation photos reveal an attractive young woman apparently in possession of an uncommon level of maturity and confidence. (Some of her serious expression may be attributed to the nature of portrait photography and limitations of camera equipment at the time.)

Ruth graduated in the heydays of the Roaring Twenties at a time when many young women wore their hair in a "bob" and engaged in frivolous nightlife activities. However, there was nothing frivolous about the way she clutched her books close to her chest in her graduation year photos. Her demeanor suggests a candor, honesty and forthrightness which probably made her well respected. There was no caption under Ruth's Vassar yearbook photo, but had there been one, it might have read "Future Teacher."

In addition to her fortuitous timing, given increasing numbers of women voting and gaining professional recognition, Ruth's achievements could be viewed as the natural progression of a young woman raised in a Midwestern family that valued higher education, a woman who envisioned a substantial and contributory future for herself.

WWI was in the past, and the confident, well-bred Ruth, a young woman with a romantic spirit, playful wit and a serious nature was finally on her way. And her path led her immediately after graduation to Springville, New York where on June 3, 1926, at age 22, she married Charles Wright Larabee.

Who was the young man responsible for winning Ruth's heart? What does his past reveal about Charles Larabee and her ultimate attraction to him?

Above, left to right: Georgia Oriana Robertson, Ruth's mother, c1900; and Charles A. Baird, Ruth's father, c1900; both in Ann Arbor, Michigan.
Below: Ruth Baird is pictured in the bottom row, second from right, in her high school sophomore year at The Barstow School.

Above left and right:
Photos of Ruth Robertson Baird
in her senior year at Vassar College,
in 1926.

Below right:
Charles Baird with Ruth's sister
Mary Baird Cunningham.
She holds her oldest child Susan
Mary Cunningham.
c1936, location unknown.

The Baird family home in Kansas City, as it appears in 2017.
This red brick mansion on a wooded estate near Loose Park
was Ruth Baird's childhood home in the early 1900s.

CHAPTER 2

FATHERS AND SONS

*Someone once said that every man is trying to live up to
his father's expectations or make up for his father's mistakes.*

— BARACK OBAMA, THE AUDACITY OF HOPE

Charles Larabee also grew up in a wealthy Midwestern family with roots in banking. The name Larabee was and still is prominent throughout Kansas, particularly in the town of Stafford where the esteemed Larabee men were considered that city's forefathers. Their arrival in 1886 was heralded on the front page of the *Stafford County Democrat*, the local paper, which announced, "Mr. J.D. Larabee of Springville, New York is in town looking up a location for a banking house. We welcome him and hope he may conclude to locate."[14]

Charles' grandfather John Delos Larabee had established a modestly successful career in New York as a cheese buyer when he moved his family to Stafford, Kansas in 1886 and began building a family fortune. He wanted to provide his two

15

college-educated sons, Frederick Delos and Frank Sheridan Larabee with the opportunities to succeed financially, looking to the mid-western United States to realize his dream.

That dream was indeed realized, but not entirely because of J.D. alone. The family patriarch established Farmer's Bank and brought in the region's first telephone and electrical system. But the big break came thanks to his two sons. In 1898 the local flour mill in Stafford suffered considerable financial reverses, and Farmer's Bank took it over to protect its loans. Although finance was the primary interest of the Larabees, the two sons eased into operating the mill so successfully that for a time it outshone the bank's prestige.[15]

Frederick Delos Larabee, Charles Larabee's father, eventually became president of Larabee Mills centered in Stafford, Kansas. It was the nucleus of their family success, a whopping enterprise that employed much of the town, spread to many other Kansas locations and into South Dakota and Missouri. At the turn of the last century, the Larabee family had climbed the rungs of the industrial elite, becoming one of the wealthiest milling families in the nation.[16]

In 1932, Larabee Mills merged with another milling company to become Commander-Larabee Corporation, with its headquarters in Minneapolis, Minnesota. *Time* magazine referred to it as "Commander to the Gulf." Larabee Flour was the third largest flour milling company in the United States in 1932, behind number one General Mills and number two Pillsbury. One of its best known brands was Air Fairy cake flour, a competitor of General Food's Swans Down.[17] Indeed, Larabee Flour cemented the family claim to fame and fortune.

Clearly Charles and his younger sister Angeline were raised in an environment that viewed money as a symbol of success. Theirs was a family living the quintessential American dream. Their father had worked hard for his fortune, climbed the corporate ladder and fulfilled his own father's wishes.

The measure of Frederick's success was recorded at the time of his death in 1920 when his corporation employed two thousand people and had a daily turnover in excess of $250,000, or what would amount to approximately $3 million in 2016 dollars. The flour empire had mills at Wellington, Marysville and Hutchinson, Kansas, Clinton and St. Joseph, Missouri, and Sioux Falls, South Dakota. Larabee owned approximately two hundred grain elevators in Kansas, Oklahoma, Nebraska and Missouri, in addition to 110,000 acres of Kansas wheat land. The Larabee men were involved in lead mining, built an iron foundry, operated a charcoal plant in the Ozarks, and built the largest cement plant in Mexico, which they sold to a British syndicate for one million dollars.

Charles' father Frederick was also considered a man of the people, and his obituary celebrated this view of him. "In surveying expeditions and inspection tours, Mr. Larabee took 'pot luck' with his employees, sleeping on hillsides at night and setting the pace in accepting hardships and risks."[18]

CHARLES LARABEE WAS born on March 22, 1901 in Kansas City, the first and only son of Frederick and his wife May Wadsworth. Imagine what it must have been like for Charles to grow up in a corporate family with an industrial titan for a father. What were the familial expectations placed on the only son of the Larabees, the heir apparent to the family conglomerate? Unfortunately, little is known today about those formative years, but it's easy to imagine that young Charles felt a great deal of pressure to succeed, to get high marks, to make something of himself and prepare to assume his father's family business when the reins were handed to him. Frederick's brother, Frank, became the President of Farmer's National and had only daughters, so there were no cousins to challenge Charles' taking the helm at Larabee Mills.

At sixteen Charles attended Western Military Academy in Alton, Illinois, perhaps in grooming for an officer position in service during World War I, although ultimately he did not serve in the war. Instead he went to Babson College, a business school in Massachusetts.

In the spring of his sophomore year Charles got a real taste of adventure. He interrupted his studies and set off either by train or boat to the port of New Orleans. From there he boarded a vessel owned by the United Fruit Company bound for San Juan, Puerto Rico. Charles was visiting Puerto Rico and Cuba on a prospecting venture on behalf of Larabee Mills to determine the possibility of developing trade with Latin America. The trip to these islands in the Caribbean was the beginning of his love affair with Latin American cultures, particularly in later years with Mexico.

With little information about this time in his life we are left to wonder what Charles thought about this overseas assignment, whether deep down inside he believed that corporate life and the flour business were his calling, or if he harbored doubts and had his heart somewhere else entirely. Was he miscast in the corporate world? Were his family's expansiveness, expensive tastes and pride in their wealth attractive to him as well?

For his passport application in 1919 Charles described himself as "5 feet 9 inches tall, with a high forehead, brown eyes, red hair and a light complexion." His photo presents a serious-faced young man in glasses with his hair parted in the middle and combed back, wearing a suit and tie typical of the fashion of the times.[19]

Passport photos have a notorious reputation of being unflattering, and his demeanor conveys the impression of a man who is slight and insecure. Is it possible Charles had misgivings about where his life was taking him? Maybe he felt ill-suited as an engineer or trapped under the weight of his father's high expectations.

If indeed that were the case, Charles' feelings of obligation—of the expectation that he must follow in his father's footsteps—might have been reduced by events in the coming year. His father Frederick died in their home in 1920 at age 57. His obituary states that he died "from peritonitis following operations on the nose," a rather unheroic death for a man of such stature.[20]

This could have been a pivotal event for Charles Larabee. His father's death, tragic and untimely as it was, meant that Charles might have to be prepared to step up to a leadership position, but on the other hand he faced the prospect of immense wealth with which to follow his own dreams, whatever they might turn out to be.

The "millionaire mill owner" F.D. Larabee left behind a sizeable inheritance for his wife and two children. One newspaper account described the amounts revealed during the probating of his will as follows:

> The two children of Frederick D. Larabee ... will not come into their inheritance until one is 30 and the oth-

er 35 years old. The will … leaves the bulk of the estate, said to be valued at one million dollars, to the widow Mrs. May Larabee, and two minor children, Charles W. and Angeline Larabee … The son and daughter are to receive one-fourth each, that of the son to be held in trust until his thirtieth year, when he will receive one-half, the remainder on this thirty-fifth birthday."[21]

The inheritance from his father of $250,000 would amount to $3 million in today's dollars. Charles had to wait eleven years to receive his first distribution, but clearly the roadmap for his future changed and his prospects for financial stability were firmly established.

THE LOCAL NEWSPAPER ran a story about Charles in 1923 which provides some insight into his personality at the time. At the tender age of 22, Charles was the victim of what ought to have been a frightening armed robbery that took a surprising and amusing turn. "Charles Larabee Took Receipt When the Robbers Left," announced the publication:

> Two dapper young bandits left a receipt for $200, after holding up Mr. and Mrs. C. Reid Murray and C.W. Larabee, of the Larabee Flour Mills Corporation of St. Joseph, Mo., guests at the Murray home here last night, taking furs and a travelling bag valued at $2,500. The bandit who calmly wrote the receipt in the living room

of the Murray home at Mr. Larabee's suggestion asserted that he made it small 'to protect the insurance company.'

Mr. Larabee opened the door to confront the two
young men who backed him down the hallway with a
pistol into the living room where the Murrays sat. The
bandits ordered Mr. Larabee to be seated. One remained to watch the victims while the other bandit
searched the house for valuables.

'How much money have you got here?' asked the bandit who remained in the living room. 'Not much,' said
Mr. Murray. 'I just wanted to know,' said the young
man. 'That fellow upstairs might hold out on me.'"[22]

Was it bravery, naiveté, or his business school background
that emboldened Charles to ask for a receipt from a pair of
robbers holding him at gunpoint? (Or had the newspaper re-
porter taken liberties with the story?) Either way, this episode
provides an amusing glimpse of the young man's character.

Right: Frederick Delos Larabee,
Charles' father, c1900,
Kansas City.

Below: Charles Wright Larabee,
age 18, from his passport
photograph in 1919,
Kansas City.

CHAPTER 3

COMING TOGETHER

Gravitation cannot be held responsible for people falling in love.
How on earth can you explain in terms of chemistry and physics
so important a biological phenomenon as first love?
Put your hand on a stove for a minute and it seems like an hour. Sit with
that special girl for an hour and it seems like a minute. That's relativity.

— ALBERT EINSTEIN

The questions of how and where Ruth and Charles met and what their courtship was like remain largely unanswered. They did, however, live near each other as young adults. In 1920 Charles lived in his family home with three servants at 52nd Street and Belleview Avenue in Kansas City, Missouri, and this was less than a block from Ruth and the Baird family home at 814 West 52nd Street. It was not uncommon in those days—when people were more homebound and transportation was not easily available—for a young man to meet and marry a young woman who lived nearby. The future

Mr. and Mrs. Charles Larabee may have met while out for a stroll or at a local café. Ruth later mentions that her mother, Georgia, met and liked Charles, and since Georgia died in 1923, the young couple must have been courting by or before that date.

Their courtship may have begun when they discovered how much they had in common. Both Ruth and Charles were descendants of powerful men in the banking business. Both were raised on estates in upper class Midwestern neighborhoods in households in which servants were the norm. Each attended a private prep school rather than a local public school. Each came from what would have been considered a small family at the time, Ruth with a sister and brother and Charles with only one sister. And each was a first born child bearing the weight of the family's hopes and dreams and high expectations.

LIKE MANY OTHER young romantics of the time, Ruth and Charles delayed their wedding until she had a proper college graduation and then wasted no time in sealing their vows. However, there were issues to overcome with regard to Ruth's father, Charles Baird, which can be seen in her lengthy correspondence with him in the spring and summer of 1926.

Now fulfilling the roles of father, mother and business professional, Charles Baird was determined to find the very best for all of his children, especially his first-born Ruth. They exchanged many letters in 1925 and 1926 while she was at Vassar, with Ruth corresponding by hand and her father sending replies that were typed and carbon copied by his business secretary. In one letter in the spring Ruth apparently informed her father that she was changing her plans following graduation, and that she and Charles wished to be married immediately. Charles Baird was full of misgivings and was thoroughly displeased with this turn of events. Fundamentally he was doubtful about her choice of a life mate. He repeatedly questioned her judgement, was concerned about Charles Larabees' ability to provide for his daughter, and worried about Ruth's level of dedication to her studies.

In a letter written May 15, 1926, Ruth pressed for understanding from her father. She hoped he would believe that despite the time she was spending with Charles, she was firmly committed to graduating from Vassar, and she pleaded for his consent to a marry despite his disapproval of the arrangement:

> Please don't worry more than usual about my work, that is the main thought on my mind—I have all my long papers finished and am studying hard for the exams. Just wasting two days. Charles and I are going to Aunt Cornelia's for Sunday dinner tomorrow as I want her to meet him.

> I am writing you about all this now because I don't want you to think later that I have not been frank. I am quite sure that I do want to marry Charles, so I am not going to take the trip abroad.

> I know you disapprove entirely and whether you believe me or not, it pains me very much. I hate to disappoint you and I find it hard for myself to have to go against you. However, I feel that this is the time, for

once in my life, to show a little force, and stand by my decision."

Ruth knew her father was concerned about whether Charles could support the two of them, whether he had the means and planning to do so. In the same letter, she wrote:

> You think that Charles has the wrong ideas about things and you don't know how good or bad a business man he is. Fortunately, I feel about things just the way he does. Of course, I am totally ignorant about business but I believe in his judgment.
>
> I hope without any reason that you will give me consent to let me marry him in time even though you disapprove. I am old enough to take the consequences of my folly. You can trust me not to bother you afterward if I act without your approval. I am not changing and I will stick to my decision and take the consequences."

The nature of Charles' business plans is not recorded anywhere in her correspondence, so we are left to wonder what he had in mind which caused Ruth to trust his judgment and require them to arrange a hasty wedding. Her father replied to Ruth on May 19 expressing his concerns and doubts about this union, writing:

> Upon my arrival home, I found your letter of May 15th. It comes at a time when I am overwhelmed with obligations and responsibilities, which cannot easily be laid aside for the present. My work touches activities

concerning many people, which cannot be disregarded now. Therefore, I cannot go East this week. Your letter surprised and grieved me because of its tone. The thoughts did not come natural to you and I feel as if you wrote the letter at a time when your mind and feelings were no longer under your own control. Your sudden change of plans, without consideration of consequences to others, involving a sudden marriage, very shortly announced, leads me to believe that you are not acting in accordance fully with your own will and reason.

Surely you cannot but think that your happiness and welfare is nearer and dearer to me than that of anything else in the world, except the happiness and welfare of your brother and sister. I am father and mother to you now and your future welfare is my chief concern.

It is impossible in this letter to go into details and discuss such a momentous subject, and I shall not try to do so. However, I am earnestly asking you to let this matter stand in abeyance until I can have an opportunity to visit and talk with you fully.

I have made my plans to spend several days with you prior to graduation and we will then have an opportunity to discuss this subject which is fraught with such great consequences to you in the future. Certainly, with all my love for you, I cannot believe it is wise for you to arrange for a hasty and precipitous marriage even before we have had a chance to talk together. Surely all the training of your mother and me and the influence asserted upon your character by the people who have surrounded you all your life will cause you to pause and think and not act in a hasty and rash manner. Again, I urge you to lay no plans until we meet."

Ruth was apologetic to her father, but despite his objections she was undeterred. She and Charles resolved to marry, on short notice to all, on June 3 at Charles' mother May Larabee's family home in Springville, New York.

Few family members were in attendance. Neither of Ruth's parents was present at the event, her mother Georgia having passed away three years earlier, and father Charles missing either because of business conflicts that couldn't be rearranged on such short notice, or because he was fundamentally opposed. Among those present was Ruth's aunt, Cornelia Larabee, a resident of New York who had played a significant role in Ruth's life up to that time, especially when Ruth was attending boarding school nearby. The groom's father, Frederick Larabee, had died in 1920, and it's unclear if his mother was able to come.

Ruth described the wedding to her father in a letter on June 12, written while she and Charles were still in Springville:

> My marriage might have been very sad in any other circumstances—I love my family and home and they were in my thoughts during the ceremony but it was so beautiful to stand in the parlor full of lilacs as Mr. and Mrs. Larabee had done, even to the same hour. We had a Presbyterian minister whose wife is a Vassar woman.

Sheridan Wait and his sister were with us, Charles had played with them here as a little boy. Their father knew four generations of the family on each side just as the old man who gave us our license did. We had a wedding cake and drove in to Buffalo with the Waits. We stayed at the Statler that night. I feel that no other man in the world would show such tenderness and surely it is wonderful to be able to love and respect each other as deeply as we do from every point of view."

In the same letter, Ruth again expressed her hope that Charles Baird would forgive her, writing:

I am fully aware of my complete lack of consideration—have always felt such conduct was unpardonable and I marvel that I ever actually acted so. It is true that your reaction is adequate punishment—even a husband is expensive at the price of losing a Father.

I hope you will forgive me some day anyway and I wish most earnestly that you could do it now. Life is short and misery devours time. I can only say that I am sorry from the depth of my heart that I hurt you so. It was not willfully done. I was simply too weak to struggle with you. It may seem more inconsiderate to tell you how happy I am. Charles is, too, and this seems the only excuse.

I am happier than I have ever been, no, more, looking to the future, but completely content with the present. I loved Charles when I married him but a week has made my love so much greater. It is perfect happiness to be with him and every breath we draw is congenial.

We have been so happy hearing from his family about old times, picking wild flowers and riding about this beautiful country in the foothills of the Allegheny Mountains.

If you cannot forgive me now, perhaps you can sometime. Try to believe I do love you and regret my meanness. It would be a great joy to have you like Charles. It is a consolation to feel that Mother did."

NOT LONG AFTER their controversial wedding, Ruth and Charles Larabee embarked on what would become their first adventure as a married couple. They packed their bags and headed west to live with Charles' widowed mother May Larabee and his sister Angeline in Hollywood, California, presumably to undertake Charles' business plan alluded to earlier. A move such as this—leaving the conservative confines of the Midwest and virtually disappearing on the West Coast—would have been considered somewhat radical in the early 1920s.

Over the course of several letters to her father and her brother James, Ruth never mentioned specifically what Charles' business venture entailed, and to the reader their goals were ambiguous at best. They moved around the Los Angeles area several times, the last time to Culver City, in order, as Ruth explained, "to be closer to his work." At one point, rather mysteriously she wrote, "The Italian has left," and later, "Charles and I slept in the factory last night, in order for him to learn to use the dryers."

Again we are left with speculation about Charles' exact occupation based on these cryptic references. However, it's possible to conclude that Larabee may have been in textile manufacturing, during a time when the fashion and fabric industry were on the rise in Culver City and greater Los Angeles. Whatever the case, the plan did not ultimately appear to have been successful. Ruth and Charles stayed in the L.A. area for only one year, then returned to Kansas City, where he worked as an engineer in milling, (though not with Larabee Mills) and she as substitute teacher in the public elementary schools.

TWO YEARS INTO their marriage, the Larabees seized on another opportunity for adventure, this time embracing their mutual fondness for boating and outdoor exploration. In the fall of 1928 they embarked on a pioneer-style voyage, an 1,800 mile boat trip which earned them a photograph and an article in the *Lincoln State Journal*. The photo caption read:

> Mr. and Mrs. Charles W. Larabee of Kansas City, Mo., leaving the dock at Michigan Avenue and the river, Chicago, in their eighteen foot boat, in which they arrived in Chicago from Kansas city by way of the Missouri, Mississippi and Illinois Rivers, the Illinois and Michigan Canal. They will return by way of Lake Michigan, Green Bay, Wolf River, Lake Winnebago Canal and the Wisconsin, Mississippi and Missouri Rivers, completing a trip of 1,800 miles."[24]

The shadowy newspaper photo shows what might be called a yacht, albeit a very small one. Ruth and Charles are in the cabin of the two person flat-roofed wooden craft, motoring into the Chicago Harbor while proudly flying the American flag. Ruth indulged her natural affinity for water, and together they began to chart their course as trailblazers.

THE LARABEE'S FIRST home in Kansas City was a charming one-story house valued at $9,000. It had a gabled roof, white clapboard siding, green shutters, a red brick fireplace, a wide front porch and a small picket fence.[25]

Sometime in the early 1930s their passion for plants literally began to take root. They turned their attention to their personal garden, which gradually gained a reputation of its own. Photos of azaleas and peach trees in bloom in their front yard were later considered significant enough to be saved in the Missouri Valley Special Collections portion of the Kansas City Public Library.[26]

Around the time Charles received the first half of his inheritance, he discontinued working in milling, and along with two friends he became co-owner of a nursery in Kansas City, appropriately named The Garden Shop. The shop comprised four acres, with trees, shrubs, evergreens, and perennials.[27]

His dramatic career change may not have come as a complete surprise. There may have been some foreshadowing of Charles' newfound interest and change of heart from heavy industry to plants and nurseries. Among other things, he and Ruth had spent the brief time in Hollywood and the Los Angeles area at the beginning of their marriage. Even though

Hollywood became synonymous with the film industry, for decades it was a largely agricultural community famous for its citrus groves and flowers. Perhaps being in the presence of so many growers and their exotic plants inspired him to become involved in agriculture-related business himself.

DURING THESE EARLY years in their marriage when they lived in Kansas City, Ruth developed some friendships that would end up lasting a lifetime. One of her closest friends, Ingaborg Midgley, faithfully recorded her own day to day activities in her personal diaries, and many of these entries included Ruth. She joined Ingaborg for tea, for luncheons, for dinners at a favorite Italian restaurant, and for lectures at the Kansas City Art Institute, a college of art and design. In September 1940 Ruth arrived with a "baby bonnet, flowers, home-made cookies and perfume" to celebrate the arrival of Ingaborg's new baby girl.[28]

With good friends, teaching, managing the nursery and gardening, life was full for Ruth and Charles. They created a delightful place of their own in their shared hometown and immersed themselves in learning all they could about Midwestern gardening and horticulture. They carved out their own lifestyle, one that was very different from their parents and unique in its own way.

In fact, Larabee Mills and all it represented was a mere memory for Ruth and Charles. No babies arrived, but they may have consoled themselves when Charles received that first half of his inheritance in 1931—$125,000, or roughly $1,500,000 in today's world—and would see the equivalent five years later. Almost anything was possible that money could buy.[29]

*Ruth Larabee at far right with friends and family, in 1933, Kansas City.
Left to right: Martha A. Williamson, Ruth's sister Mary (Baird)
Cunningham, Mark Cunningham and daughter Susan Cunningham,
Ingaborg (Williamson) Midgley, and Ruth Larabee.*

CHAPTER 4

THROUGH A DIFFERENT LENS

Around here, however, we don't look backwards for very long.
We keep moving forward, opening up new doors and doing new things,
because we're curious ... and curiosity keeps leading us down new paths."

— WALT DISNEY COMPANY

In the late 1930s, Charles had the time and resources for his artistic side to bloom. He invested in a camera, outfitted a darkroom for himself and began developing a body of work in large format (16 x 20 inch) black and white photos which won him awards and recognition and later became collectors' items.

His interest in photography began with high school and college photo club activities and contests. Charles garnered Awards of Merit for his photographic series of construction workers in high rise buildings. Later his work matured and grew in importance based on trips to Mexico and Central and South America where he lived and travelled months at a time, leaving Ruth to keep home fires burning and gardens tended.

Several of Larabee's early photographs reflect the Gothic influences typical of the Art Deco era and the rise of Hollywood movies, with dramatic lighting, deep shadows, strong contrasts and sharp angles. Acclaimed photographers of this time on the leading edge of experimentation included Americans Edward Weston and the young Ansell Adams.

Other photos in the late '30s collection focus on a very different motif: Mexican ranchers driving cattle, farmers plowing their fields, field hands transporting water on their backs, oxen plodding along centuries old trails, and Navajo Indians performing the rituals of their everyday lives. Some of these photos were exhibited in the Kodak Building at the New York World's Fair in 1939.

Larabee's subject matter shifted again when he developed an interest in horse and cattle ranching and documented the fading cowboy culture in his black and white compositions. This phase of photos included ranch hands branding their herds, rodeo riders, the classic rider-less horse gazing out to the horizon, and other motifs that glorified the myth of the American cowboy.

Larabee himself dressed the part—in plaid shirt, bandana, a Stetson hat, and sometimes a pipe. He engaged in film and photo lecturing on the Arizona/Utah canyon country, Monument Valley, and the tribal life of the Navajo Indians.

San Diego nature photographer Nicholas Paoni, whose images have been published in *National Geographic* magazine and on the *National Geographic* "Your Shot" website, commented on Larabee's skills illustrated by the following four photos:

> The lone rancher is a proud and handsome figure, and his eye contact with the photographer is exceptional.

Larabee chose a diagonal slant rather than an upright, more rigid posture for his subject. In doing so, he portrays the rancher in a more relaxed state, looking directly at you. The background is handled well with no clutter in it, nothing to draw your eyes away from the rancher.

In the photo of a village in Central or South America, Larabee made excellent use of the frame in the lower left quadrant, filling it nicely with the townspeople. From there the eyes can track upward and to the right where you see the relationship of the people to the buildings in their village, and then to the left where you see their relationship to the landscape. It's a wonderful presentation of the villagers both within their village environment and their natural environment.

The photograph of ranch hands branding their stock is very entertaining. In the foreground you see the ranchers in the process of branding, but there is a lot more than this to absorb your interest. The framing is very deep, enabling you to see other activities, like the men standing around and a horse in the background. So while your attention is primarily drawn to the main subjects in the lower left quadrant, your eyes can also explore interesting elements throughout the frame and then return and rest again on the foreground.

Lastly, Larabee used portrait framing for the composition of the boats anchored next to the cliff. This allows the viewer to get an excellent impression of just how big this cliff actually is. If he had only included the cliff we would have no idea how big it is, but including the boaters and the water off to the left of them is a clever way of giving the viewer perspective on the size, scale and grandeur of this river scene."

Through his camera's lens and in his darkroom Charles Larabee recorded lifestyles that were worlds apart from his own and which had a profound effect on him. He looked at poverty and primitive living conditions in Latin American cultures. With his artistry, he captured the moods, beauty and wonder of remote locations and historic sites and recorded a unique chapter in the history of America's final frontier.

THOSE CAMERA SKILLS earned Charles an invitation to the trip of a lifetime. In 1940 he joined a group of six men two women on a commercial two-month voyage down the Green and Colorado Rivers in Utah. In maneuverable cataract wooden rowboats constructed by boatman and veteran explorer Norman Nevills, they wound their way through 1,463 miles of rapids and mesmerizing Grand Canyon scenery.

Also along for the ride was the accomplished photographer Barry Goldwater, Jr., (later a Senator of Arizona and Presidential candidate) who published a book about the adventure entitled *Delightful Journey*. He wrote:

> In 1940, I fulfilled a lifetime ambition to explore by boat the Green and Colorado Rivers (before the river was dammed and controlled.) In a lesser and latter-day

sense the journey duplicated the boat trip of the intrepid one-armed explorer Major John Wesley Powell ...
when he and his nine companions entered the cascades
and rapids, hearts in their mouths."[30]

In his book, Goldwater described Charles as an "affable
fellow," and Nevills said of him, "Our photographer was C.W.
Larabee of Kansas, a genial and excellent all round man."[31]

Charles and his companion "river rats" travelled in the
three small boats primarily by rowing, occasionally turning on
the motors in between rapids. The intrepid explorers left the
river just three times in two months in order to resupply. During the rest of the trip they camped on rocky or sandy shores
deep inside the Grand Canyon.

"There were eight of us, including two women, and we
breathed sighs of pleasure and anticipation as I gave the signal
to push the three rowboats into mid-stream," wrote Nevills.
"Over 1,000 miles of canyons and rapids were ahead of us—
scenery to hold the most critical among us spellbound."

Accompanying Nevills, Larabee, and Goldwater were
Nevills' wife Doris as the cook, Dell Reid, a prospector, B.W.
Deason, a Salt Lake City assayer, J.S. Southworth, a California
mining engineer, Anne Rosner, a Chicago school teacher, Mildred Baker of New York, and Dr. Hugh Cutler, a prominent
botanist at the Missouri Botanical Gardens. (Some of the party
travelled only part-way and traded places with others. Whereas
there were more than eight voyagers in total, only eight were
actually aboard at any one time.)

Botanist Cutler had joined the party with the stipulation
that he would be free to collect plants along the way. It was
during this trip that he made his first archaeobotanical discov-

ery—some corn cobs that he recovered from an Anasazi ruin along the river which were about 900 years old. This find launched his career-long groundbreaking research into ancient varieties of corn or maize.

"Early each morning, Doris would write a resumé of our previous day's events and send the message to the Salt Lake City newspapers by carrier pigeon," wrote Nevills. "On a few occasions film was sent out this way, and a few hours later the pictures were printed in the newspapers."[32]

Goldwater, Cutler, and Larabee were sailing partners in the boat named *Joan*, and Goldwater recorded their experiences numerous times in his book. On July 10, 1940 he wrote, "… Hugh and Charlie and I decided that the falling waters of the geyser, near the Green River, would make an excellent shower bath, even though the water stinks in (sic) high heaven." On July 17 Goldwater noted, "Charlie's duffel and bedding were soaked by the rain in the *Joan's* back compartment yesterday, and last night's shower did not help them dry any faster, so we got a late start this morning … waiting for his things to dry out."

On August 5, "Today Charlie and I are sleeping on top of a rock to escape the blowing sand that has bothered us for many nights," and on August 8, "Charlie, Hugh and I stood on the banks of the Colorado River … and marveled at the great mass of Chuar Butte, upstream near the junction of the Green and the Colorado."

Goldwater's August 12 entry said, "Norm Nevills permitted Charlie and me to run the last two boats, *Mexican Hat II* and *Joan*, through Hermit Falls …. Charlie and I have had good luck on all we have run." On August 18, "Charles and I have put our sleeping bags in the creek bed. This is the dumbest place in the world to sleep, especially when a rainstorm is in the offing .... We selected this spot because of its softness, telling ourselves we would hear a flash flood approaching."

True sleep, the most basic of creature comforts, was a rare commodity on the adventure. Goldwater remarked ruefully, "I have slept on ledges, on rocks, on sand, and in cow dung; I have slept dry and wet; I have slept hot and cold, and before man and beast and the Old Boy, *it ain't sleeping*. It's just lying."

Overall, however, as Goldwater summarized, "The opportunity for this type of adventure has to an extent been eliminated by progressive upstream development of the river ... and I feel privileged to have gone down the river at a time when the journey was still a great and rare adventure."[33]

A charming profile portrait of Larabee taken by Barry Goldwater during the trip has him squinting into the sun, with full beard and mustache and a scarf and bolo around his neck. He tilts his head up to absorb the warmth. His pose is reverent, soulful, like someone having a spiritual or religious experience. Charles indulged in an increasing number of adventures like these from which Ruth was noticeably absent as the years went by.

Larabee in his darkroom in Kansas City, c1938.

Church of Santa Tomas in Chichicastenango, Guatemala, c1938.
Photo by Charles W. Larabee.

Rancher in Mexico, c1938.
Photo by Charles W. Larabee.

*Townspeople in a village in South America,
most likely Bolivia or Peru, c1938.
Photo by Charles W. Larabee.*

Ranch hands branding a pig, location unknown, c1940.
Photo by Charles W. Larabee.

*The Colorado River adventure began at the Green River, Utah,
in July 1940. Charles Larabee stands second from left,
and Barry Goldwater, Jr., is seated second from right.*

Barry Goldwater, Jr., running the rapids near Lake Mead, 1940.

*Larabee takes a moment during the Colorado River trip
to absorb the sun, 1940.*

Charles Larabee as a self-styled expert on the American Southwest, c1941.

CHAPTER 5

WE'RE NOT IN KANSAS ANYMORE

Twenty years from now you will be more disappointed by the things you
didn't do than by the ones you did do. So throw off the bowlines.
Sail away from the safe harbor. Catch the trade winds in your sails.
Explore. Dream. Discover.

—MARK TWAIN

Toto, I've a feeling we're not in Kansas anymore.

—DOROTHY, THE WIZARD OF OZ

Precisely what drove Ruth and Charles Larabee to pick up stakes and move west in the early 1940s remains a mystery. There are no letters or journals that explain their decision, no Larabee descendants to tell the tale. The few people still alive who knew them haven't a clue about what inspired the Larabees to leave Kansas City, nor do they know why the two made a remote ranch on a hill in Encinitas, California their new home. In a way, the Larabees seemed oblivious to the drama playing out in the rest of the world at the time. In the early 1940s the greatest conflict in human history—World War II—was raging, and the Depression still affected countless numbers of people all around the globe.

Maybe Charles' fascination with the American Southwest and their earlier taste of California living in the Los Angeles area steered him toward one of the last western frontiers. Perhaps the Larabees' passion for trees and flowers led them to an ideal environment for growing plants, just 43 miles from Mexico and its wonderland of new and exotic species. Since Charles was a nurseryman he may have heard that Encinitas was progressing as a haven for plant growers and collectors.

Whatever their reasons, Ruth and Charles lay claim to two remote parcels of land and a rustic ranch and put down their new roots.

IT WAS RUTH Larabee who signed the deeds and paid for the two properties. In December 1942 she purchased ten acres of land from a single man named Herman Seidler, a German immigrant who purchased the land parcel in 1923 while he was a temporary boarder at the Ecke Ranch. This parcel included a large shed and small cottage.

In June 1943 Ruth purchased the adjacent 16.5 acres with a small ranch home and barn owned by Anton van Amersfoort, an experienced avocado grower. Together these two pieces of Southern California land formed the new Larabee estate, and cost Ruth approximately $11,000. As they had set out to do, the Larabees now had a genuine stake in one of the last American frontiers.

RUTH AND CHARLES planted themselves in the midst of what was soon to become "The Flower Capital of the World." The neighboring coastal towns of Encinitas, Cardiff and Leucadia underwent an exciting transformation beginning in 1923 when Paul Ecke, Sr. arrived, the grower responsible for popularizing poinsettias for the Christmas holidays at his ranch next door to the Larabees. The steady migration from Los Angeles brought more and more flower growers to this area, as explained by Robert Melvin, in *Profiles in Flowers: The Story of San Diego County Floriculture:*

> A new breed of farmer began to appear. These pioneering horticulturists were, by and large, experienced nurserymen with an outlook that went well beyond the supplying of local markets. Their orientation was toward the large wholesale fresh flower trade ... and the bulb market nationwide. These new growers leased farm land, planted all the acreage they could afford, prayed for the right weather and hoped for a profit when the crop was sold. They came from all over the United States, Canada, Europe and even the Orient to grow flowers in the fertile soil of San Diego County.... With their vast acreages of blooms, these . . . growers brought a new dimension to local agriculture and established a floriculture industry that remained an important part of San Diego County's economy for years to come."[34]

The Larabees had indeed picked an exhilarating time to arrive in Encinitas. It was an important period in the history of

American horticulture, and many of their neighbors worked at the leading edge of horticultural experimentation.

San Diego's North County also possessed a unique sociology, one which had a considerable Hollywood influence. Perhaps this was of added interest for Ruth and Charles Larabee. The celebrity culture was particularly evident in the early to mid-1900s, with silent screen stars like Mary Pickford and Douglas Fairbanks making their homes in the area, and movie actor Leo Carrillo's rancho was just a few miles from Encinitas. The Del Mar Race Track attracted stars like Bing Crosby, Jimmy Durante, Lucille Ball and Desi Arnez, who made the local community their second home. Whether or not Ruth and Charles casually befriended any of these people or were in the least drawn by the excitement they lent to the local culture is pure speculation. Nevertheless, it was a fact of the times in which they arrived.

THE NEW LARABEE homestead sat on a much eroded ridge of sandstone belonging to the so-called Del Mar Formation, one mile from the coast overlooking the Pacific Ocean to the west and backcountry and mountains to the east. The ranch enjoyed the moderate influences of westerly breezes from the Pacific, and its canyons and bluffs created micro-climates supporting southern maritime chaparral and a small portion of coastal sage scrub.

Southern maritime chaparral is a threatened habitat that grows along the coast only from southern Orange County to the tip of San Diego at Point Loma. It is associated with coastal fog and eroded sandstone soils and is characterized by plants like black sage, chamise, coast scrub oak, prickly pear cactus, and yerba santa. A number of rare species of plants are found, including the federally endangered Del Mar manzanita.

Coastal sage scrub, on the other hand, is found from San Francisco south into Baja at low elevations, primarily on mesas within fifteen miles of the coast. Typical vegetation includes coastal sagebrush, black sage, California buckwheat and lemonade-berry.

All of this vegetation provided a haven for wildlife that Ruth enjoyed. The ranch was a bird watcher's delight, with quail, ducks, hawks, woodpeckers, road runners, hummingbirds and towhees among the dozens of species spotted around the ranch. With several coastal lagoons nearby, the occasional egret or heron also dropped in. Lizards, grey foxes, rabbits, snakes, coyotes, opossums, bobcats and skunks were frequent but not always welcome guests.

RUTH WAS FASCINATED by the "Legend of San Ysidro," about a Spanish saint who was venerated as the patron of farming. He lived a life of hard work and charity on a farm near Madrid until his death in 1130. Legend says that an angel ploughed his fields while he prayed, rewarding his piety. His image is carried in procession through the fields as a blessing for a good harvest on his feast day of May 15th.[35]

Ruth was also particularly fond of flowers, and before long she combined the two images and named their home "El Rancho San Ysidro de las Flores," or "The Ranch for Farmers of Flowers."

The term "ranch" or the Spanish "rancho," (a small Mexican ranch) was part of the local vernacular in those days. Even though it implies a large farm where livestock is raised, (like actor Leo Carrillo's nearby 2,500 acre Rancho de los Kiotes,) everyone in San Diego's North County—including Ruth and Charles—was in the habit of referring to his homestead as a ranch, even if there were very few animals present. And why wouldn't they? This was still to some degree considered the western frontier, and that was part of the thrill. Most of the owners were not in the livestock business typical of traditional ranches, but it was their mentality or state of mind that mattered. Short of having a hitching post and bleached cattle skull out front, the Larabee property was a California ranch in the language of the time, expressing their notions of the American West experience.

SOME OF THE Larabees' new property had already been cultivated by their predecessor Anton van Amersfoort (1881-1973). He had immigrated to the United States from Holland and came into possession of the Larabee property through a foreclosure sale at the sheriff's office in 1923.

The deed to the property was put up as security on a loan taken out by J. Frank Cullen, his wife Esther, J.H. Parker and Donald Carlton Ingersoll, but Carlton and his wife Gertrude were the actual owners. J. Frank Cullen came from Boston to the West Coast and proceeded to develop the town of Cardiff (or Cardiff-by-the-Sea). His wife Esther was of Welsh decent and she wished for all the streets to be named after places in Great Britain. Thus the streets are named Birmingham, Manchester, Nottingham, Glasgow, Edinburg, and so forth. Cullen also built Cardiff Elementary School, one of the earliest schools in the area, which is still in operation today.

Ultimately the group of four defaulted on the loan, so the court ordered the property to be sold through auction, at which point van Amersfoort saw the opportunity and seized it.[36] Over time, he became a major landowner with a claim to at least 16 different properties in the general area, one of which was as large as 80 acres.

In relatively short order, van Amersfoort became a well-recognized avocado rancher, listed in a 1928 Avocado Growers' report that mentions he planted 11 acres of avocados in Encinitas in 1919. The report complimented him by saying:

> About one-half of the orchard is planted to the Fuerte variety, with perhaps ten per cent each of Queen, Dickinson, and Anaheim and miscellaneous for the others. That Mr. van Amersfoort could bring this orchard through four years of dry farming and now have it in such excellent condition is a tribute to his understanding of tree growing. He is a strong advocate of the excellence of the Fuerte variety."[37]

Van Amersfoort also cultivated avocados on what later became the Larabee ranch. The primary access to his home, running north from San Marcos Drive was called Amersfoort Drive. (San Marcos Drive is now Encinitas Boulevard, and Amersfoort Road was changed to Quail Gardens Drive.)

In addition, he was a prime mover in the local water district when irrigation finally did come on the scene in 1923. Van Amersfoort was a director of the Encinitas Water District (which later became the San Dieguito Irrigation District) and held this position for a number of years, even surviving a recall petition. It's likely he graduated from dry farming and had water lines installed at his ranch with hose bibs to irrigate the avocado grove and plantings around the house and barn.

The industrious Dutchman was clearly interested in land development and sales and likely had the monetary means to enhance the value of his property through landscape improvements. He had a hand in convincing the Larabees in 1943 that the ranch would be a good real estate investment and had landscaped it pleasingly enough to attract their attention. Since Ruth and Charles were newcomers to the challenges of California horticulture, van Amersfoort probably also showed them how to water and maintain the plants.

Van Amersfoort lived as a bachelor on the ranch for 20 years and married his wife Tunnie sometime after he left. During his stewardship he demonstrated the expertise necessary to successfully plant and establish a number of species in addition to avocados. Though there are no official records of these plantings, snapshots taken by some of Ruth Larabee's Camp Fire Girls, combined with aerial photos from 1939 and 1949 indicate the presence of non-native trees that were too large to have been planted in the first six years of the Larabees' occupancy and thus were probably van Amersfoort's contribution.

These include the following: California pepper tree, *Schinus molle*, red ironbark, *Eucalyptus sideroxylon*, red flowering gum, *Corymbia ficifolia*, river red gum, *Eucalyptus camaldulensis*, sugar gum, *Eucalyptus cladocalyx*, Torrey Pine, *Pinus torreyana*, and weeping bottle brush, *Calistemon viminalis*.

Van Amersfoort planted rows of trees on either side of the curving lane leading downhill from the house to what is now Quail Gardens Drive. Most of the trees were Monterey cypress trees, *Cupressus macrocarpa*, but several red flowering gums, *Corymbia ficifolia*, and olives, *Olea europaea*, were also planted. Unfortunately many of the cypresses later succumbed to canker disease. Today only the hollowed trunk of one of the Monterey cypress trees remains along with one red flowering gum.

Takeo Sugimoto, a young boy who lived nearby across Saxony Drive described van Amersfoort as "jolly." But this particular jolly Dutchman had considerable drive, talent and ambition, and ultimately carved out his own significant place in the history of what was to become San Diego Botanic Garden.

THE LITTLE HOUSE on the Larabee ranch was built around 1918 by Donald Ingersoll, a rural mail carrier and car repairman who got into the development and construction business with J. Frank Cullen. Ingersoll and his wife Gertrude (later called Nana by her grandchildren, and nicknamed "Nan" by her friends) purchased the property in 1917, and built a barn in which they temporarily lived until the house was completed in 1918. They stayed there until 1923 when van Amersfoort took ownership. Originally the one-story ranch home was 1,024 square feet in size, with a rustic wooden exterior and interior and doors that opened directly into the living room from the front and back. Beyond the living room there was a kitchen, bedroom and bath.

Ruth and Charles added some Midwestern elegance and style to the living room by installing wood paneling and built-in bookcases on either side of the fireplace, trimmed with thin molding in a curving design typical of the 1940s. They plastered the walls and edged them with wood wainscoting.

Overall, the living room was darkly lit and furnished with antiques Ruth and Charles had inherited. It was decorated with ethnic art, some from Mexico, some Navajo in origin. The Larabees were especially fond of blackware, or black-on-black pottery created by the internationally known Native American artist Maria Martinez and had several of her pieces in the living room. Martinez was from the San Ildefonso Pueblo near Santa Fe, New Mexico. After years of experimentation, she rediscovered the lost art of black-on-black pottery, an ancient process that required tremendous patience and skill.

Ruth had a sunburst patterned quilt on the four-poster bed and a yellow milk-glass lamp at the bedside. She decorated the bathroom in a sea motif. And the Larabees' wedding china, which was Spode's "Ermine Blue" pattern, was tucked away while they lived at the ranch.

The ranch included a two-horse barn down the hill in what is presently the Lawn House. In that building, the present day living room was the hay loft, and the horses were stabled immediately below. The only other structures on the property were a large green shed and a tiny cottage. And that was the extent of the "estate" where Ruth and Charles found themselves, on a sparsely settled coast which was a far cry from the Kansas City mansions in which they had been raised.

Above:
Donald Carlton Ingersoll, c1915,
and Gertrude Ingersoll, c1920,
original owners of the Larabee
House, from 1917 to 1923.

Right:
Anton van Amersfoort, c1900,
avocado grower who lived in the
Larabee House
from 1923 to 1943.

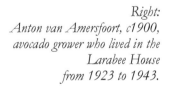

CHAPTER 6

GROWING THE NEXT GENERATION

*If a butterfly flaps its wings in Brazil, it might produce a tornado
in Kansas. Unlikely as it seems, the tiny currents that a butterfly creates
travel across thousands of miles, jostling other breezes as they go
and eventually changing the weather.*

—EDWARD LORENZ, "FATHER" OF CHAOS THEORY

Eventually it became clear that Ruth and Charles Larabee
were not destined to have children of their own. By the
time they were middle aged, that ship had passed them by.
Maybe that was an added incentive to pack up, move west and
make a new start. A few years after they were settled at their
new home, however, it was clear they both craved the experience of young people in their lives for numerous reasons,
among them the chance to share the outdoors and the many
ways in which it enriched their own lives.

Becoming involved in youth organizations ultimately sat-
isfied that need. Ruth held multiple positions involving youth
groups. She was leader of a troop of Senior Girl Scouts from
about 1946 until 1949 when they graduated from San Dieguito

High School. She was also one of the area's first summer day camp directors, overseeing young girls' outdoor activities at Glen Park in Cardiff-by-the-Sea. And in about 1950, she became the camping sponsor for the Wananka Camp Fire Girls, a position she held for several years. Charles was Scout Executive (next in line to Scoutmaster) for Explorer Scouts, a senior division of Boy Scouts, from around 1946 to 1949.

Both Ruth and Charles were fully immersed in this new chapter of their lives, befriending the young men and women wholeheartedly, almost as surrogate children. Ruth already had experience as a teacher and was a natural leader. With this new endeavor she continued to share the wonder of nature with a younger generation.

For the dozen or so Senior Girl Scouts and around fourteen Camp Fire Girls, the 26-acre ranch was the perfect place to earn badges and beads, to absorb nature and free their imaginations. Youth meetings were frequently held at the ranch, usually outdoors, but occasionally they sat in front of a fire in the living room.

Ruth welcomed the girls whenever they were around. Former Girl Scout Connie (Conrad) Lund lived downhill and across the street to the east of the Larabees and she and her friends felt comfortable riding their horses up onto the Larabee property. "Ruth was quiet and reserved, and very patient with us. She knew that we rode horses around here a lot, and she didn't seem to mind at all," she explained.

Ruth's troop of Senior Girl Scouts was referred to as "the exclusive troop," according to Janet McNulty, whose own mother led the Brownies and Juniors. "While the other troops were scraping for pennies, the Larabees paid all the expenses for her troop." This included financing their camping trips to

Borrego Springs and Cuyamaca Rancho State Park, high desert and mountain regions about 90 miles east of San Diego, to Ensenada, a coastal city 78 miles south of San Diego on the Baja California Peninsula, and to Santa Catalina Island, off the coast of California southwest of Los Angeles. Charles always accompanied Ruth and the girls, and typically their mode of transportation was the back of the Larabees' pick-up truck or Charles Larabee's yacht, which he kept in Orange County.

"Mrs. Larabee never got flustered, she was very calm and never cross or uptight," said Lund. "She didn't do any kidding around. She was very serious, but sweet." She remembered Ruth always insisted that the high school girls put zinc oxide on their noses as sunscreen.

Ruth was also regarded as someone who was not the least bit "flighty," a comment made by Gerald Cullison. "She was a very down to earth, solid person," Cullison observed, "and she demonstrated that through all her activities with the Girl Scouts and Camp Fire Girls."[38]

The combination of these characteristics and others—her overall reliability, fortitude, intelligence, determination, and love of the outdoors—equipped Ruth well for the responsibilities of a troop leader. In 1949 the Girl Scouts headed 60 miles north to Newport Beach, California, where they boarded Charles' yacht for a trip to Santa Catalina Island. Unfortunately, it was an outing that confirmed the worst of a troop leader's fears. Connie Lund described the event:

> The Larabees took us to Catalina Island to spend the night. When we got there Betty Harris complained that she didn't feel well. We thought it was because we had been sleeping on the floor. She complained the whole

65

day—we had just barely arrived—and eventually they called the doctor over and found out she had polio. We were put back on a boat … and were quarantined for two weeks at different houses. Even though Mrs. Larabee was a calm person, that made her cry."[39]

Polio had been occurring in epidemic proportions in the U.S. for several decades. Perhaps its most famous victim was President Franklin Delano Roosevelt. Infants, children and young people were more susceptible than adults to the truly virulent disease which left its victims with paralysis in the legs, arms, and/or diaphragm. Sometimes it was fatal.

Treatment at the time of the Catalina trip included quarantine of the patient and any people who may have been exposed. In the most severe cases of polio, people were enclosed in the infamous iron lung, a giant metal tube that helped weak and gasping patients breathe.

The episodes of polio peaked in 1952 when 58,000 new cases were reported and 3,000 Americans died. The following year Dr. Jonas Salk announced the discovery of an injectable polio vaccine that was finally determined to be safe and effective in 1954. Millions of children were automatically vaccinated upon starting school. By 1957 only 6,000 new cases were reported. In 1962, Albert Sabin announced the availability of an oral vaccine which is so commonly used now that the terror which the possibility of contracting polio struck into every parent's heart has almost been forgotten.

AFTER SEVERAL YEARS with the Girl Scouts, Ruth switched to Camp Fire Girls, the youth group that was most near and dear to her heart. According to former Camp Fire Girl Marcie Phillips, "Ruth's aunt was a life-long friend of Dr. and Mrs. Luther Gulick, founders of the Camp Fire organization, and she sponsored one of the first groups in the country, which was in Kansas City. As soon as Ruth was old enough, she became a member, and there was never a more enthusiastic Camp Fire Girl." Ruth eventually earned the rank of a Torch Bearer.

The Camp Fire organization's long-held traditions based on Native American history and culture still resonated for Ruth as an adult. In a letter to gladioli hybridizer Elizabeth Briggs, also a Camp Fire leader, she wrote, "I believe that next to a girl's religion, Camp Fire can be the greatest influence for good in her life." Phillips remembered Ruth saying that gardening, working with girls, travel, reading, studying birds and getting letters from friends gave her great satisfaction, "but Camp Fire was her first love."

Ruth's introduction to the Wananka Camp Fire Girls was thanks to Mary Carol Isaacs, a resident of nearby Rancho Santa Fe who met Ruth at a League of Women Voters meeting. Like Ruth, Mary Carol was an ardent Camp Fire Girl as a child. In about 1950 she organized the local Encinitas club and was leader of around fourteen young women, including her daughter Kathy. Ruth became the camping sponsor and was also responsible for ceremonies.

"She was somewhat of a trail-blazer as far as young women were concerned," remarked Gail Petty, a Camp Fire alumna. Gail's mother Beth Ann Byers Stone was a leader at about the same time as Ruth Larabee. "She was very supportive of young women's rights, abilities and talents at a time when her community's attitudes were very conservative in this regard."

Carol (Hasselo) French, one of the Camp Fire Girls, recalled a time when they camped on the Larabee ranch and

67

cooked a most unusual dinner in the "ovens" or fire pits that Charles dug into the hillside:

> We went for a walk to Olivenhain and hiked up to what is now the backside of Lake San Marcos Dam. On the way we came across a rattlesnake. It was about six feet long and we killed it with clods of dirt. Mr. Larabee cut it up, skinned it, floured it and cooked it, and we each had a piece of that rattlesnake. It reminded me of chicken and rabbit."[40]

This story illustrates how safety standards—particularly for children—have changed dramatically over the years. Current trail practices recommend giving a snake wide berth, avoiding sudden movements and walking around it, and certainly do not recommend pummeling it with clods of dirt, no matter how large.

Marcie Phillips added a juicy tidbit to the rattlesnake story. "We fried the rattlesnake in bacon grease left over from breakfast. We didn't notice that grease ants had gotten into the bacon fat, so our dinner was full of little black specks. But we were campers at heart, and we convinced ourselves it was pepper."[41]

Kathy Isaacs' little sister Caroline was four years old at the time the club was formed and also became acquainted with Ruth as her mother's friendship grew. Though she was not one of the Camp Fire Girls, Caroline became a frequent visitor to the Larabee House. She remembers staying there a few times in the mid-50s when her family was out of town. "One time Ruth sent me to Bible school," she recalled with a chuckle. "I was never sure if that was intentional or she just needed to find something for me to do." Caroline was entertained by Ruth Larabee's two small dogs, whose names "Sabado" and "Domingo" meant Saturday and Sunday in Spanish.

Through thick and thin, Ruth developed deep bonds and lasting friendships with the young women and their mothers, like Mary Carol and Caroline Isaacs, and Connie Lund. She stayed in touch with many of them in the years that followed. "This always amazed me," Connie Lund reflected. "There was one time when there were a few of us at my house and the phone rang and it was Ruth Larabee. I passed the phone around so she could talk to everyone. It was particularly special because we were adults by then, I was married and she lived in Kansas City."

Ruth continued to look in on Connie and her new husband when she was in the area. The Lund family purchased the home which belonged to Helen Woodward, the local philanthropist who founded the Helen Woodward Animal Center in Rancho Santa Fe, California. "The house was on the beach in Del Mar," Lund explained. "Helen was going to have it torn down and hauled off. So we paid to have it moved … and reassembled it on Crest Road in Encinitas. Ruth stopped by often to look at our house and see what we were doing with it."[43]

Ruth Larabee was a major force in shaping the lives of all these young women. She encouraged their personal explorations, taught them survival and decision making skills, helped them make friends and build self-esteem. Most of all she awakened in them a lifelong love for nature and wildlife that they would treasure for years to come.

CHARLES LARABEE'S APPROACH to scouting was as different from Ruth's as they were different from each other. While he and Ruth were mutually fond of the outdoors and seemed to be natural teachers, his gift to the Senior Explorer Scouts Troop No. 774 (sponsored by the Encinitas Rotary Club, in which Charles was a lifetime member) was uniquely his own: it was raw adventure.

Many of the scouting adventures he shared with the Explorer Scouts stemmed from his renewed interest in white water river boating. Charles parlayed the skills he acquired during his 1940 Colorado River trip into creating a small side business guiding river excursions later in the 1940s. Initially he collaborated with Norman Nevills and used his wooden boats. Later he partnered with Harry Leroy Aleson, a pioneering river guide of the Colorado Plateau, to create the "Larabee-Aleson River Tours."

The two first met in 1940, then ran into each other again by chance years later when they arrived at the Rainbow Bridge in Utah from separate expeditions. "A partnership was formed as they sat and talked beneath the great multi-colored span of stone which is Rainbow," *The Desert Magazine* reported in September 1950. "Charles Larabee likes the river, and accompanies the boat trips when his business affairs will permit, but Aleson is the managing partner who pilots the expeditions and arranges the details."

Aleson particularly liked the thrill of using power boats to up-run the rivers and rapids. Most often he and Larabee deployed Army Air Corps 10-man rubber boats, which they ultimately discovered to be superior to Nevills' wooden crafts.

In 1949 Larabee ran a promotional announcement in *The Desert Magazine*, a monthly regional publication focused on the desert country of the Southwestern United States and Northwestern Mexico. It read, "Charles W. Larabee has announced that he will make passenger boat trips down the San Juan River from Bluff, Utah, to Lee's Ferry, Arizona." These were billed as eight-day trips amid the scenic canyons of Southern Utah, with visits to Rainbow Bridge National Monument—one of the world's largest natural bridges—and "other points of interest in this magnificent canyon country." In 1949 he scheduled four of those trips. In the same year Larabee and Aleson offered seven passenger trips through Glen Canyon, Colorado. As an added attraction they included "two days in Monument Valley at Harry Goulding's Navajo trading post."[45]

Charles was fast becoming a self-styled expert on the American Southwest, and the Explorer Scouts were the lucky beneficiaries of his knowledge and reputation. Former Scout Doug Hasselo remembers that the troop made the inaugural voyage of Larabee-Aleson Tours, sailing down the San Juan River to the Colorado River and stopping to hike around the Rainbow Bridge. "Another year we went down the other side on a 15 mile hike," he related. "We went through the bottom of the proposed Marble Canyon Dam. We also hiked through the Grand Canyon and spent a couple of nights at Phantom Ranch."[46]

Larabee was widely known and well regarded throughout these parts. And his friendship with one person in particular—the legendary Ernest Thompson Seton—greatly influenced his beliefs and character as a mature man.

Former Scout Richard Cullum explained:

> Charles took us on trips to places we had never been
> before. And it seemed like everywhere we went on
> boating trips there was somebody important there who
> knew Charlie. On one occasion perhaps 1946—we had
> just arrived in Canyon Duchesne, Utah—it was raining
> and this man rushed over to meet us, and asked, 'Are
> you Charles Larabee? Wow!' Toward the end of that
> trip we met up with Ernest Thompson Seton, one of
> the founding pioneers of Boy Scouts of America who
> invited us up to his ranch. He greeted us with great
> hospitality and gave us a tour of the house. He was
> sick at the time, yet he wanted to see us because of his
> relationship with Charles Larabee. He treated Charles
> like a step-son."[47]

How fortunate that Charles was treated like "a step-son"
by this living legend. The English born Ernest Thompson
Seton (1860-1946) was a co-founder of Boy Scouts of America. He was responsible for the strong influence of American
Indian culture in the Boy Scouts and was the author of the
first *Boy Scout Handbook*.

But Seton's legacy extends far beyond the Scouts. He was
also one of the country's leading nature writers and illustrators
as well as a noted scientist and conservationist. He is recognized, along with William Bartram, John Audubon, John Burroughs, and John Muir, as one of America's most influential
naturalists, and is credited with being a seminal figure in the
emergence of the American conservation philosophy in the
early twentieth century.

Seton used his influences to push for the creation of more national parks, and he personally lobbied for environmental legislation. He believed that people had to care about the wilderness in order to respect and save it, and he breathed new life into this country's appreciation of nature.

Ernest Seton was a pioneer of the modern school of animal fiction writing and wrote and illustrated over 80 nature and wildlife inspired books. His most famous is entitled *Wild Animals I Have Known*, published in 1898. This book earned him the friendship of President Theodore Roosevelt, and his literary friends included Mark Twain. The storyline of one of his animal sagas was the inspiration for the 2009 PBS television documentary entitled, *"The Wolf that Changed America."*[48]

Envisioning an "academy of outdoor life," in 1930 Seton established a 2,500 acre ranch in the foothills of the Sangre de Cristo Mountains of New Mexico. Here he built not only a castle for his family, but a village, a children's camp, a printing press and a teaching and cultural community that focused on his interest in wildlife conservation and Native people. Seton Village developed as friends and colleagues settled together with a common vision. Among Seton's associates were members of the Santa Fe arts and literary community during the mid-1930s and early 1940s, including such luminaries as painter Georgia O'Keefe. Seton Village is most likely where Charles Larabee and the Explorer Scouts visited him, and since Cullum remembers Seton as being in poor health, this was probably just shortly before he died in 1946.[49]

The expression, "You can learn a lot about a person by the type of friends he has," applies to Charles Larabee's close relationship with Seton. Perhaps some of the time he lingered in the Southwest was to visit this eminent man. He undoubtedly looked up to the charismatic Seton as a father figure and absorbed many of his teachings and ideals. Charles probably shared these ideals with Ruth, and the Seton influence likely spread to her experiences with the Girl Scouts and Camp Fire Girls as well.

THE OUTGOING CHARLES Larabee enjoyed sharing some stories of his own and imparting a bit of wisdom whenever time allowed. "He did a lot of talking on our trips, all kinds of philosophy of life," recalled Cullum. "He talked a lot about William Jennings Bryan," Cullum noted, "and mentioned that the Larabee family had invested in a lot of silver." Bryan was a Nebraska Congressman and a populist democrat who ran three times for President of the United States and served as Woodrow Wilson's secretary of state. He was also the lead prosecutor in the famous "Scopes Monkey Trial" in 1925. Bryan believed that since gold was in insufficient supply, it was an inferior metal on which to base America's currency. He promoted silver instead because it was more widely available in American mines.

When they weren't boating, the Explorer Scouts met in what they called "the Barn" on the Larabees' ranch (also the Scout Hut at the time, and now known as the Lawn House.) "It was just a bare room," Hasselo said. "I don't know if Larabee used it much at all other than for Scout meetings and sometimes the Camp Fire Girls."

But the Barn was fabled for an exotic treasure hidden within its walls: the legendary shrunken head. Former Explorer Scout Jack Ambriz told Julian Duval, "I used to stay on that property and take care of it when the Larabees went away. If you look very hard I'm certain you will find the genuine shrunken head that Charles brought back from his travels in South America."

The practice of human head shrinking originated in the Amazon Rain Forest and was largely done for trade or religious purposes. Westerners discovered the grisly heads and created an economic demand for these souvenirs in the early 1900s. The trend peaked in popularity around the time when Hollywood movies were featuring exploits into forbidding jungles. Fortunately, purchasing the shrunken heads was later banned altogether.

Bob Gooding, another former troop member, confirmed that the gruesome souvenir actually did exist. "The shrunken head was in a glass case," he said, "and sometimes Ruth allowed it to be in the house. At first she didn't, but later she did. The only person I ever knew who had such a thing was Charlie. If it was available, he was likely to have it." Perhaps Ruth finally got her way and banished the dreaded head to an afterlife in the dark recesses of the Barn.

In any event, Duval said, "We never found it of course. We never really looked for it. But then in 2012 we came in contact with Charles Larabee's step-son by a second marriage, Bill Hopkins, and discovered that, lo and behold, there really was a genuine shrunken head! He said it was one of the creepier things they had around the house when he was a teenager. Hopkins told us he ultimately sold the shrunken head for the tidy sum of $10,000."[49]

THE TIES FORMED between Charles Larabee and members of this younger generation were lasting ones, just as they were for

Ruth. Several recalled keeping in touch with "Charlie" in later years when they were young adults.

Bob Gooding, one of those who kept in touch, has fond memories of his Scout experiences and said he considered Charles Larabee to be an excellent and generous friend:

> I cherished the thought of being an Eagle Scout in that troop, which was unusual at the time since it was a small group. A few years later, I went to borrow some money from the bank in Encinitas. I was a refrigeration engineer at the time and had been in the Coast Guard. I came out of the bank and Charlie Larabee stepped up on the curb and asked what I was doing with all those papers. He said, 'Come by the house, I'll give you a check for the loan.' It didn't matter how much. He gave me the check, and eventually of course I did pay him back. Charlie was a really thoughtful person."[50]

Gooding said he was "endeared" to the Scoutmaster, a man named T.C. Spruitt, and the "Scout Executive," who was Charles Larabee.

Ruth and Charles were united in their belief in the ideals behind scouting, its roots in Native American cultures and respect for the land. And through scouting the Larabees were able to "parent" the younger generation in rich and meaningful ways. They invited these young people into their lives—lives which were by no means perfect, but which were driven by their attachment to the natural world. The steady-handed Ruth with her intensity and dedication, and the affable Charles with his bold and generous spirit established a tradition of inspiring young people to interact with plants and nature that remains a hallmark of San Diego Botanic Garden today.

Above: Girl Scouts pause while loading the truck following their camping trip in Borrego Springs, California, c1947. Ruth stands at the far left.

Below: At the end of the Borrego Springs trip, Ruth and Charles tie down the baggage. Note the girls riding in the back of the pick-up truck.

Above: Girl Scouts aboard a medical boat, following the ill-fated trip to Santa Catalina Island in 1949. Ruth Larabee stands mid-center.

Below: Charles Larabee in the Encinitas Rotary, early 1940s. Larabee is in the bottom row, far left.

A Larabee-Aleson guided river trip in the Southwest, c1949,
which may be the trip the Explorer Scouts were on.
Photo by Charles Larabee.

Mothers and daughters in the Camp Fire Girls meet with Ruth outside the Walled Garden at the Larabee House, c1950. She sits in the center facing the camera. The car by the porch was Ruth's automobile.

Former Scouts and youth friends gather for lunch and memories at the Larabee House in 2012.

Above, left to right: Caroline Isaacs, Lola (Roach Larson) Gooding, Connie (Conrad) Lund, Jan Bittner, Sally Sandler (author,) Mel Bittner, and Dave Ehrlinger.

Left: Bob Gooding.

82

*Additional guests at the 2012 luncheon, left to right: Ruth Cullum,
Richard Cullum, Doug Hasselo, and Carol (Hasselo) French.*

CHAPTER 7

TRANSFORMING THE RANCH

"If you look the right way,
you can see that the whole world is a garden."

—FRANCES HODGSON BURNETT, THE SECRET GARDEN

El Rancho San Ysidro de las Flores meant everything to Ruth. In her garden on the hill she found herself and lost herself almost every day. By all accounts it was her joy, her therapy, her raison d'être. People who knew Ruth during the time she lived at the ranch knew this about her: she was out when the sun came up each day, making the world a more beautiful place.

"She was quite a remarkable gardener," remembers Caroline Isaacs. "She would be out at dawn, training plants to grow just the way she wanted them to. When you look at the acacias at San Diego Botanic Garden you can see how she formed them. The way she pruned and shaped them was an art, something you could never forget."[51]

In their early years at the ranch, Ruth and Charles were probably equally involved in the whirlwind of activities that surrounded plant collection and landscaping. After the mid-1940s, however, Charles' white water river boating adventures and other activities drew him away from the ranch for long periods of time so he likely didn't participate in the garden as much as Ruth. As time went on, it was Ruth's hands that were in the soil and her mark left for posterity.

To get that hard work done, Ruth adopted a no-nonsense approach to dressing which typically consisted of her trademark overalls, a T-shirt and boots. She tamed her dark waves in a coiled braid around the back of her head or by gathering them into a "snood," a hairnet attached only to the back of the hair, not the entire head. This was considered more stylish than a full hairnet and was quite popular during the WWII era with women entering the workforce.

"She looked beautiful to me, even though she never wore makeup," former Camp Fire Girl Marcie Phillips commented. "But those green rubber boots she usually wore with her overalls were too big for her, so they made a squelch-squelch sound as she walked towards you."[52]

Transforming the degraded old pastures and croplands into gardens required much more than overalls and work boots. About a third of the property was the avocado grove and old barley fields and another third was former pasture and disturbed areas, so the Larabees' work was clearly cut out for them. The remaining third was Southern maritime chaparral which they decided to leave unspoiled for wildlife habitat.

SINCE BOTH RUTH and Charles were drawn to Latin culture, they began the hard work of transforming their ranch by making some changes to the outside of their home that reflected the Spanish Colonial Revival architecture made popular in San Diego in the early 1900s. They enclosed the back yard with a white-washed adobe wall with rustic carved wooden gates, punctuated by a Moorish arched window opening and trimmed with blue and white Mexican tiles. Together with the dwelling's low slung appearance, the large open front porch, and many of the existing trees—like the California pepper tree, *Schinus molle*, and weeping bottlebrush, *Callistemon viminalis*— these improvements transformed the ranch into something more like a rancho, the overall effect evoking California's historic Spanish mission roots.

A photograph from Caroline Isaacs taken around 1950 illustrates how the Walled Garden looked about seven years after the Larabees arrived. At that point the whitewash was fading off the adobe brick wall, lending it an ancient, time-worn appearance.

Whitewashed adobe bricks were also used to build ornamental details at each side of the entrance by the road, which were more decorative than functional. These roughly two-foot high structures created corners for the path of grass leading into the Walled Garden but were not raised beds themselves. Tucked in and around these decorative features, Ruth's charming flower gardens were well under way.

IRRIGATION ON THE ranch was initially a daunting task. In addition to irrigation heads installed by van Amersfoort in the avocado grove, Ruth and/or her hired help probably extended hoses from hose bibs installed by van Amersfoort to hand water various plantings. But legend has it that Ruth also sometimes dealt with irrigation by hauling buckets of water up the hill from the nearby Cottonwood Creek. As unlikely as it seems, she probably did resort to this method of irrigation for special trees that were outside the reach of a hose, particularly those on the lower east side of the property.

Cottonwood Creek was very close by. It originated at the pond on the corner of what is now Leucadia Boulevard and Quail Gardens Drive, nestled in the ranch property that was owned by Encinitas settler Edward G. Hammond and his family in the late 1800s. Hammond's seven children enjoyed cooling off in the pond on hot summer days. From there the creek meandered south and west roughly parallel to and about 100 yards downhill from what is now Quail Gardens Drive.

To locate the former creek, consider this: The drive created by Anton van Amersfoort ran from the house downhill past the barn and crossed what is now Quail Gardens Drive. The eastern portion of this dirt road is now called Mays Hollow Lane. The south-running dry bed from Cottonwood Creek can still be seen among the willows crossing Mays Hollow Lane, just yards from the entrance to San Diego Botanic Garden. Ruth could have easily scooped up creek water there in years with good rains. Eventually Cottonwood emptied into the Pacific Ocean at Moonlight Beach in Encinitas. Early settlers in the area could be seen washing and hanging their laundry there, near the mouth of the creek.

Records indicate that before Ruth Larabee left Encinitas in 1957, some of the watering issues had been solved using irrigation and sprinkler heads. One appraisal noted 67 lawn heads used for the "formal gardens," and 230 rotary heads for the avocado grove.

ALMOST EVERY GARDEN presents its owners with a learning curve, and even with the help of professionals, the Larabees sometimes gardened by trial and error just like everyone else. One day Marcie Phillips paid a visit to Ruth and found her working side by side with her Mexican employees in the Walled Garden, which seemed to have been her exclusive domain. "She was kneeling in the dirt when she looked up and saw me. 'Oh, Marcie,' she said, 'when I first bought this ranch I expected this would eventually be a field of chrysanthemums. Instead, all that comes up here are weeds.'"[53]

Weeds or no weeds, the Walled Garden was ready for its first official wedding by the summer of 1949, when Nancy Aker, one of Ruth's former Girl Scouts, exchanged vows with Fred Hampe. On close inspection of their wedding photos it's possible to see that this outdoor garden room was filled with flowers and plants typical of Midwestern gardens of the time, and that Ruth had planted things with which she was probably most familiar.

The adobe walls were softened with borders of flowering shrubs and trees, with clusters of perennials, bulbs and annuals in the foreground. Carolyn Isaacs remembered seeing rows of blue pincushion flowers, or *Scabiosa*. These borders were framed by African boxwood, *Myrsine africana*, and creeping fig vines, *Ficus pumila*, inched their way up the adobe bricks.

BEYOND THE HOUSE and its adjacent beds, however, an entirely different sort of garden evolved. The Larabees branched out from what was typical in their community and became fearless about trying new and unknown species. They were surrounded by the greenhouses and flower fields of the burgeoning Flower Capital of the World, with their neighbors in the business of growing and hybridizing things like carnations, gladioli, and orchids. Yet Ruth and Charles took a novel approach in the midst of this floral wonderland by amassing extensive collections of cacti, aloes, euphorbias, and shrubs and trees from Mediterranean zones around the globe, all of which were more eco-friendly and sustainable than traditional cutting flowers. To do this, they developed a network of seasoned professionals familiar with the landscape design and management that was unique to large estates in their region.

One of these was Clifford Tanner, a nurseryman from Rancho Santa Fe with whom Charles consulted early in their planning. To understand his probable contributions, a few words about Rancho Santa Fe are required. Located five miles inland from Encinitas, Rancho Santa Fe was originally a Mexican land grant of 8,824 acres from California's Governor Pio Pico to Juan Maria Osuna, the first mayor of the Pueblo of San Diego. In 1906 the Santa Fe Railway purchased the entire land grant from the Osuna family descendants to plant a blue gum eucalyptus (*Eucalyptus globulus*) tree plantation for railroad ties, though in the end that wood was poorly suited for such use. The railroad then formed the Santa Fe Land Improvement Company to develop a planned community of country estates.

In 1921, Lilian Rice was chosen to develop the community's master plan, working under the architectural firm of Requa and Jackson. Her inspiration for the built environment was the Spanish Colonial Revival style, and surrounding landscapes in Rancho Santa Fe developed a Mediterranean signature intended to suit this style as well as the San Diego climate.

Coming from this environment and serving this clientele, nurseryman Tanner likely brought some of these same elements of design and plant selection to the Larabees for their consideration. Tanner is also responsible for introducing the 'Vista' hybrid macadamia nut (*Macadamia* 'Vista').

Another accomplished professional consulting on the Larabee ranch was Christen Westergaard, a nurseryman who contributed many native and exotic plants to Ruth Larabee's gardens. Of Danish birth and horticultural training, Westergaard was an experienced professional in Mission Hills, an affluent neighborhood overlooking downtown San Diego which was also known for its Spanish Colonial Revival architecture and landscaping. Many of the homes in Mission Hills were designed in the early 1900s by Richard Requa, the architect with whom Lilian Rice was employed.

In 1925, Westergaard invited his cousin Walter Anderson to work at his nursery, named Rose Court Floral Company. Anderson had no previous horticultural experience, but after training with Westergaard, he opened his own retail nursery in 1928 which is a San Diego landmark today. According to Westergaard's granddaughter, Debra Judson Earle:

> My grandfather propagated from seeds and cuttings, and he was particularly interested in plants of Mediterranean nature. His growing fields were on ten acres in the Mt. Soledad area of Pacific Beach, which he purchased from his close friend, Kate Sessions, who lived nearby. Mom remembers many hours spent listening to her father and Kate discussing and exchanging information of their mutual knowledge of horticulture on Kate's porch over tea."

91

Kate Sessions, whose nursery was in Mission Hills, is San Diego's most famous horticulturist, known as the "Mother of Balboa Park." With this network of connections and influences—from Rancho Santa Fe, Mission Hills, Lilian Rice, Richard Requa, Kate Sessions, Clifford Tanner and Chris Westergaard—Charles and Ruth Larabee were linked to the larger world of the city of San Diego in terms of horticulture and landscape design.

Locally they were in good hands, too. Ruth was a close friend of Mildred Macpherson, a noted educator in San Diego's North County who was also a landscape architect and co-owner, with her horticulturist husband James, of Williams-Macpherson Nursery in Encinitas. Ruth was a frequent customer at their nursery and stocked her garden with many of their new and unusual plants.

THE LARABEES DEVELOPED the outlying gardens by using the existing Torrey pine trees planted by Anton van Amersfoort as anchors around which they grouped their new and expansive, trucked-in collections of exotic ornamental trees, shrubs and succulents. According to Dorothy Behrends, Quail Gardens Foundation Board member and Garden Editor of *The San Dieguito Citizen*, "Many of the large specimens of cacti and succulents were literally transported by Mrs. Larabee and her husband in their trucks with crews of workmen. They had the necessary permission to take them from Mexico as well as permission to bring them into California."[54]

Through their combined efforts, and with Ruth's continuing zeal and creativity, "The Larabee home became a showplace for a remarkable, vast collection of plants," wrote

Dale Wood, editor of the first edition of *Quail Call*, the park newsletter, in 1964. "Few of their plants were common. Some were downright rare. And many fine specimens that they had collected dated from the early 1920s."

By 1957, those areas that were landscaped were botanical showstoppers, lavishly planted with over 200 different species selected for their ability to survive in the local climate and conditions. Many of the more rare succulents had attained unusual size under their care. In addition to succulents, their collection featured fruit trees and native plants. And still, plenty of acreage was left untouched as native habitat for the quail and other wildlife. (For a complete list of plants from the Larabee era, see Appendix B.)

One of the most unique trees planted under Ruth's supervision was the dragon tree, *Dracaena draco* which is silhouetted in the logo for San Diego Botanic Garden. (For the dragon tree, see Appendix A: Today at San Diego Botanic Garden.) According to Julian Duval, "Ruth commissioned T.C. Spruitt, the Scoutmaster, to plant the grove of dragon trees in the Canary Islands area. He found a woman in Del Mar, eight miles south of the ranch, who had a number of small plants, dug them up and transplanted them on the Larabee ranch where they still stand today."[55]

A native of the Canary Islands, the dragon tree is a muscular looking succulent that can grow over 50 feet tall and live over several hundred years. Sap from the dragon tree is a distinctive reddish orange color. Legend has it that this sap was used to create the trademark red stain applied to the Stradivarius violin.

Arguably the most elegant trees on the property planted by Ruth Larabee are the cork oaks, *Quercus suber*, which line the sidewalks leading to the center of the garden with their graceful, open canopy, signature bark and copious acorns. (See the cover of this book.) Cork oaks have a storied past, in part because they are native to countries in the western Mediterranean like Spain, Portugal, and Morocco, and of course due to their association with wine. During the middle of the 20th century, there was also a high demand for cork in the western world since it was a crucial insulator for the defense industry's wartime production of planes, ships and equipment. But supplies were threatened by Hitler and the Axis powers, and at one point it was thought that our access to cork would be completely severed.

For years during WWII and after, Arbor Day celebrations across the U.S. featured governors and other officials intoning to live and radio audiences how citizens could help keep America "free" by planting a cork oak tree. The Forestry Department urged everyone with available space to plant them. Initially this movement—deemed the "Cork Oak Project"—was designed by private business owners in the cork industry. But it grew legs, and in response to the need, 4-H groups, Boy Scouts and garden clubs requested the seedlings and planted trees to do their patriotic duty. The Larabee's cork oak grove apparently originated from one such seedling from Spain, planted by their landscape architect Clifford Tanner. After it produced acorns, the seedlings were cultivated, and today twelve impressive offspring grow as a result.

Sometime in the 1950s Ruth also acquired the stunning sapphire tower, *Puya alpestris*, which is native to Chile. Its unearthly, metallic-looking, deep turquoise blooms are highlighted with bright orange anthers, looking like nothing else in the plant world. For a flower lover from the Midwest like Ruth, this would have been a knockout discovery.

ABOVE ALL ELSE, Ruth was particularly fond of the coveys of California quail that dashed around her ranch. She was enchanted by the handsome little California state bird with its rich gray colors, intricately marked chest and curious forward-drooping head plume. Its stiffly accented "Chi-ca-go" call was a familiar sound in the chaparral and bushy areas outside her house. Gerald Cullison reflected on Ruth's attachment to the California state bird. "She loved those little birds. That was one of her dreams. The garden plants were her treasures and the quail were like family."

In 1855 California quail were plentiful and popular game birds in the western United States and were successfully transplanted to Hawaii and New Zealand. Quail were so plentiful, in fact, that they were hunted and sold to San Francisco and Los Angeles restaurants for as little as fifty cents a dozen. As many as 32,000 dozen eggs were sold in 1882 alone. At this rate of exploitation, however, and with expanding development in the 20th century their numbers began to diminish, and quail became a regulated species.[56]

So Ruth Larabee did everything in her power to foster their survival, bringing in bags and bags of appropriate bird seed. "In my opinion she brought the quail here," observed Bob Gooding. "She fed them so well on a continuing basis that they simply stayed here and didn't move on."[57] Lucille Waite, a parent who helped Ruth with the Girl Scouts, remembers, "She was absolutely thrilled when she finally got some of the quail to come right up to her feet to eat."

While Ruth indulged her love of wildlife and followed her dreams, as the decade came to a close Charles travelled more and more frequently to pursue some dreams of his own. Ruth's choices beg the question: Why didn't she travel and participate in the river expeditions along with him, particularly in view of her love for water? Perhaps she remained at the ranch in order to take care of her gardens. Indeed, her visions for the ranch of flowers were taking shape, but unfortunately their marriage was unravelling.

The first wedding in the Walled Garden took place in 1949,
setting the stage for hundreds more to come.
Note Ruth Larabee's plantings visible along the rear wall.

This photo, taken around 1950, shows the whitewashed adobe brick walls and decorative features. Ruth is bending over the wall at the right, gathering up items after a meeting with the Camp Fire Girls.

CHAPTER 8

THE DIVORCE

We ruined each other by being together.
We destroyed each other's dreams.

—KATE CHISMAN, RUN

The spring of 1949 was not a time for celebration, joy or renewal at El Rancho San Ysidro de las Flores. On the contrary, that particular spring greeted Ruth Larabee with news that dealt an emotionally heavy blow: Charles filed for divorce on April 5. They had been separated since February so it did not come as a complete surprise for Ruth, but the reality that their marriage was broken beyond repair was shattering. She and Charles had been married for twenty-two years, living together at the ranch for the last six.

Another year went by before the divorce was finalized in April 1950. As if that weren't enough, one more date was added to the record: Charles remarried in August 1950, just four months after the ink on the divorce papers was dry.

Looking at photos of Ruth in that period—with the Girl Scouts in 1949 and Camp Fire Girls around 1950—it's evident she had been under a tremendous amount of stress. Her face was so thin and drawn she was almost unrecognizable. She appeared gaunt and frail. Her clothes hung on her slender frame and her posture was stooped. It's a testimony to Ruth's courage and stamina that she was able to maintain her composure and proceed with any of the functions that were required of her during that time.

The change in Ruth's appearance is particularly dramatic in the June 1951 photo taken at the groundbreaking ceremony for the new Scout Hut. The photo is part of a dedication plaque at the entrance to the Ecke Family Building at San Diego Botanic Garden.

The story behind the photo is a happy one. Recognizing the Boy Scouts' need for more space than what their barn provided, Ruth donated 4.2 of her 26.5 acres for use by the Boy Scouts and for a new Scout building. The usual movers and shakers joined together to build an official Scout Hut. Scoutmaster T.C. Spruitt designed the building, the Encinitas Rotary Club took charge of fund raising and construction, and the Scout Hut opened in 1951. Later, Paul Ecke, Sr., a founding member of the Quail Gardens Foundation, Inc., purchased the property and in 1971 donated it to the County to become part of the gardens.

Ruth was always the first to admit she was camera shy, and the grainy newspaper photo is particularly uncomplimentary. But what's striking about it is her slumped and awkward posture, her barely forced smile, and most of all the apparent lack of confidence and pride. This was all in sharp contrast to her appearance in better days. The photo of the groundbreaking, when combined with several of the others taken in 1949 and around 1950, suggests that Ruth suffered the separation and divorce physically, emotionally and deeply.

Ruth's closest friends confirmed this by saying, "She took the divorce really hard, and she was really distraught." Others were bitter and made unflattering remarks about "that woman who lured Charles away." They said Ruth had told them that, "Charles was completely changed after he got all that money," that she didn't recognize the man he had become, referring to his inheritance of $250,000 in the 1930s.

Rumors were exchanged in hushed voices that Ruth had issues with alcohol abuse and depression which might have contributed to the break up, or been a response to the break up, or both. She might have even been cited for drunk driving at night, but such rumors were never confirmed.

Fortunately during these difficult times Ruth had many trusted allies, a network of women in Encinitas and around the country to whom she could turn for validation, who called her and treated her as "a dear and devoted friend." They would be there for her just as she had been for them in times of illness or distress. She would need those friends to help her find the strength and resolve to move forward.

Ruth Larabee is standing third from left among the other officials at the June 1951 groundbreaking ceremony of the new Scout Hut. Gladioli hybridizer Elizabeth Briggs takes the first shovel.

CHAPTER 9

HAPPILY EVER AFTER

Happiness is an accident of nature,
a beautiful and flawless aberration.

—PAT CONROY, THE LORDS OF DISCIPLINE

Happiness is having a loving, caring, close-knit family
in another city.

—GEORGE BURNS, COMEDIAN

Sometime after his separation from Ruth in 1949, Charles moved to Balboa Island in Newport Beach, California, a glamorous seaside city 48 miles south of greater Los Angeles. He lived on the scenic Grand Canal Waterway which was dotted with piers for homeowners' boats. Balboa Island was fast on its way to becoming one of the most expensive real estate markets in North America outside of Lower Manhattan.[58]

Charles' new wife was Lila Pihlblad Hopkins, a descendant of Swedish parents who was renting a place nearby on Balboa Island. Lila was divorced from William Hopkins and had custody of her two teenaged children, Bill and Jean.

Larabee told his new step-son that he had met Lila at a dinner party at his home at 227 Grand Canal. Charles was a music lover, and Lila, an accomplished pianist trained at the Julliard School of Music, won his heart by performing for him that night. In addition to their love for music, Lila and Charles shared similar roots: she was born in Lindsborg, Kansas, about 50 miles from Charles' hometown of Kansas City. Apparently their romance bloomed quickly. Charles was 49 and Lila 43 when they were married by a justice of the peace at Charles' home in August 1950.

Bill Hopkins quickly grew fond of his new step-father and they got along famously. Charles was easy going, gregarious, and charismatic. Bill described him as a "Renaissance man" who enjoyed music, reading, travel, fine wine, and woodworking. He made finely-crafted furniture from exotic lumber and often invited Bill's buddies and their girlfriends into his wood working shop to let them all hang out.[59] Instead of boating, Charles got his pilot's license and took up flying his Piper and Beechcraft airplanes around the southwestern United States.

Generosity was also a Charles Larabee trademark, according to Bill Hopkins. He explained that Charles lent a helping hand to another young man just as he had done with Bob Gooding:

> One of my teenaged friends came from an underprivileged background and Charles took him under his wing. He told my friend that he would pay for his college education on the condition that when the student graduated he would in turn try to send at least two kids

to college. And they would send two more kids to college, and so on. That student went on to graduate from college with a major in physics. Charles was consistently true to his promises, definitely someone who believed 'Your word is your word.'"[60]

Charles also had the gift of a sense of humor. For a short time after the divorce he continued to acquire unusual plants from Mexico for Ruth's garden, and Bill Hopkins described one of those ventures that had a comical twist:

Charles and I went down to Mexico, since he wanted to bring some plants back for Ruth. We had these plants in the car and we were worried we'd be stopped at the border. Charles decided that one way to get the plants through Customs was to put a rattlesnake in the trunk. Sure enough, when the border patrol opened the trunk the snake began to buzz, so we were quickly waved on through."[61]

In 1957 Charles and Lila took Bill with them for two months in Europe. Charles had his Bentley shipped overseas and hired a driver to escort them. They stayed for a time in a house in Spain occupied by Ernest Hemmingway when he wrote *The Sun Also Rises*, a famous novel published in 1926 about a group of American and British expatriates who travel to the Festival of San Fermín in Pamplona, Spain to watch the running of the bulls and bull fights.

The legendary glamor and gore of bull fighting pervaded Spain and was a tourist attraction for years. Charles was all about new adventures and thrills, so he took young Bill to watch a fight. The teen was so completely taken by what he witnessed in the bullring that he asked if he himself could have matador lessons. Charles promised Bill that he could, and being true to his word that time meant that Larabee not only paid for the matador lessons, he also purchased the bull.

Charles approached philanthropy with his characteristic good nature and charm. In 1957 he and Lila underwrote the construction of a new wing of the Nora E. Larabee Memorial Library in Stafford, Kansas. The library was built by Charles' grandfather John Delos Larabee in memory of his daughter Nora, who died from tuberculosis at an early age.

Charles relished the opportunity, and in his publicity photo for the *Stafford Courier* he stands beaming at Lila, a cigar in his hand, while Lila gazes back at him adoringly and the librarians look on.

Later still, they reached out to her alma mater. Lila had graduated in 1925 with a major in music from Bethany College in West Virginia (where her uncle Ernst Pihlblad was president.) Since the college was near and dear to her heart, she and Charles created a joint trust for the Music Department by transferring the interest earned from some of their numerous business properties in Los Angeles.

Larabee was also a lifetime member of the Encinitas Rotary Club and sponsored more than a dozen underprivileged local students through college.

Charles Larabee got a new lease on life when he moved to Balboa Island and married Lila. Clearly he was happy being a man of means and living large. And now it was Ruth and the ranch that were in his rear view mirror.

YEARS AFTER CHARLES Larabee married Lila Hopkins and pursued a happy and successful second life for himself, a peculiar rumor developed with regard to his whereabouts. This rumor persisted, acquiring the proportions of a myth—at least among people in Southern California—until early in the 21st century. It was the myth of the "sinking ship."

The account was shared in a speech made by Julia von Preissig, founding member of Quail Botanic Gardens and President of the Foundation at the time the park opened in March, 1970. In addition to her more traditional opening remarks, von Preissig paid tribute to the memory of Ruth Larabee, "A generous and beloved lady." And she also included the following statement in her speech:

> Both Mr. and Mrs. Larabee were known for their love of rare plants and flowers. Mr. Larabee brought back specimens from his plant expeditions into Mexico and South America and planted them here. *He later perished in the sinking of his yacht which had been used for the expeditions.*"

Suddenly Charles Larabee's history was dramatically rewritten. Instead of divorcing Ruth and living happily ever after, he now was purported to have died tragically in a sinking ship, and this myth held fast until actual research debunked it in 2010.

What's most striking is that people who were in a position to know the truth, friends and business acquaintances who were undoubtedly familiar with the real story, were in attendance at the opening of the Gardens and seem to have accepted this history as it was reported in good faith by Julia von Preissig.

Something led these friends, and many acquaintances and admirers in years to come, to allow this tragic myth to persist, almost as if to shield or protect Ruth Larabee in the public eye. Perhaps it had even been at Ruth's request.

In any event, as with so many other issues in their lives, the myth of the sinking ship, in which Charles was purported to have been the one to "come to a watery grave," goes down in the history books as one more unusual story about Ruth and Charles Larabee that will probably never be explained.

Charles and Lila Larabee (center) at the dedication
of the addition to the Nora E. Larabee Memorial Library
in Stafford, Kansas, 1957.

CHAPTER 10

THE END OF AN ERA

The need for change bulldozed a road down the center of my mind.

—MAYA ANGELOU

*I have learned that if you must leave a place that you have lived in
and loved and where all your yesteryears are buried deep, leave it any way
except a slow way, leave it the fastest way you can.*

—BERYL MARKHAM, WEST WITH THE NIGHT

*Fountain of sorrow, fountain of light,
You've known that hollow sound of your own steps in flight.
You had to hide sometimes, but now you're all right.*

—JACKSON BROWN, SINGER, SONGWRITER

After their divorce, the Larabees proceeded to divide their properties, with Ruth retaining the two parcels she had purchased that comprised her Ranch of Flowers. She may have grown accustomed to living at the ranch alone most of the time with just her two dogs for company. For some people, living in relative isolation like this would be an unnerving experience. But given her reflective, contemplative nature, perhaps Ruth had come to appreciate some solitude. And she knew she wasn't really alone, even though her closest neighbors were some distance away. On the contrary, she lived in a closely-knit community of warm and caring people, and she shared that spirit with those who continued to arrive.

Among her neighbors were Jean and Harry Schneider, who moved to Encinitas from Japan in 1950 with plans to manage a four-acre passion fruit farm to the north of Paul Ecke's ranch. Unfortunately, those plans never materialized. An uncharacteristic freeze settled over the vines, killing them all before the Schneiders even arrived.

The freeze thwarted their plans, but it didn't alter the friendship that developed between Ruth and her new neighbors. The story of this friendship reminds us of the turbulent times in which they lived during WWII and in the years that followed.

Jean was among the first Asian "war brides" to settle in Encinitas after the fighting ended. Her Japanese name was Hamako Amano. Harry was a member of the U.S. Military Intelligence Service stationed in Tokyo when they met. They were married in Japan against her father's wishes and despite all the odds being stacked against a Japanese woman marrying an American man in the military.

During their courtship, Jean showed tremendous courage in the face of daunting challenges: maintaining contact with Harry while he secretly travelled back and forth to the U.S., getting married in Japan, and then moving to America were uphill battles in every possible regard. Love won out in the end, but it literally required an act of Congress to make that happen. They were unable to go to America until congressional action HR 6271 of the 81st U.S. Congress was signed by President Harry Truman in 1950, allowing Jean and about 20 other Japanese immigrants to enter the United States.[62]

Ruth didn't waste any time in getting to know the Schneiders, inviting them up to her ranch on several occasions. "Her house was very dark and old looking inside," recalls Jean, "with very old furniture in the living room." Ruth pointed out all the flowers and trees she loved while they strolled through the ranch and down toward Saxony Drive.

In 1952 Ruth dropped by their house for a very different reason. Jean and Harry were celebrating the arrival of their first child, Esther, and Ruth came bearing gifts to congratulate them. She arrived at the Schneider's door carrying an exquisite Japanese doll in one hand and a tiny wooden doll's chair in the other. "I thought these might be nice for your new baby girl," she told Jean. Ruth had purchased the doll while travelling in Japan, and now she thought it would be the ideal gift to acknowledge Jean's heritage. The little chair appeared to be an antique Ruth had inherited since it was very well worn, its blue paint chipping away and straw coming loose from the seat. "Ruth wasn't a fancy person," Jean observes. "She was very warm, and you couldn't tell she was rich."

Jean remembers when Paul Ecke paid them a visit, too. "He was very open, so nice, and it was even more surprising to me because he and his wife Magdalena were very prominent people."

Jean had been afraid she wouldn't be accepted in America, fearful she might encounter prejudice toward Japanese immigrants so soon after WWII had ended. On the contrary, however, she was relieved to find that people like Ruth Larabee,

Paul Ecke and others in the neighborhood were welcoming and kind to her wherever she went. That spirit of acceptance was a recurring theme in the horticulture-based community that Ruth called home. Jean still lives in the same house at age 90, and continues to be grateful to have been a part of this remarkable neighborhood.

IN ADDITION TO her immediate neighbors, like the Schneiders, Paul and Magdalena Ecke and Nan Ingersoll, Ruth's circle of friends included fellow gardeners like Julia Luippold and Mildred Macpherson, naturalist Mildred Williamson, and scouting friends like Mary Carol Isaacs and Elizabeth Briggs. Other local friends included Mary Cullum, Dorothea Fox, Dolores Reyna, Willemeintje Spruitt, and Lucille Worley. Ruth spent time with a local group of women who were probably alumni from Vassar College, and sometimes she invited them to stay overnight or join her camping in the desert. Occasionally they walked from her ranch down hill to coastal Encinitas for movies at the La Paloma Theatre, a pleasant round trip of about three miles, during which at that time there were no paved or asphalt roads in sight.

She also devoted considerable time and energy to charity work. Over the years the degree of poverty she witnessed among the people in Mexico had a profound effect on Ruth, one which gradually became a calling. She sometimes requested help from former Explorer Scout Bob Gooding, who described how he assisted her in this undertaking:

> She liked to go down and help the poor people in Mexico. This was a passion of hers. Because the trans-

portation was so poor in Mexico, she would call when she got to the border and I would go get her and bring her home. Ruth and I had a working relationship. I always had a car and pickup truck—I had my own business—so I could drop everything and go get her, and she knew that. She was quite a volunteer. She helped them put up buildings, clear trash and brush. She worked like a field hand, way down in Mexico."[63]

Gooding's story doesn't explain how Ruth got to Mexico in the first place, but it reveals a great deal about her dedication to the Mexican people as well as his loyalty and commitment to Ruth. And she was not alone in these efforts. Her neighbor Magdalena Ecke was deeply involved with a Mexican orphanage, driving across the border once a month, her car "stuffed to the roof with as many essentials as she could squeeze in."[64]

Ruth was not one to spend money extravagantly, but she did indulge in travelling and had the means to do so. Details about the financial arrangements of the divorce are not available, but even if she and Charles did not split the remainder of their assets, she had inherited a fortune of her own after her father died in 1944.

Between 1951 and 1957, Ruth ventured oversees numerous times. She travelled with her brother James to Switzerland. She also flew to Cannes, Nova Scotia, England, Taiwan and Madrid. In the United States she made trips to Kansas City, Boston and various destinations in Michigan, Kentucky and Florida to visit members of the large Baird family clan.

In 1953 she visited her dear friends Ingaborg and Kenneth Midgley, which gained attention in the society column of the local paper. "Mrs. Kenneth E. Midgley was hostess at a tea this afternoon at her home for Mrs. Ruth Baird Larabee of Encinitas, Calif.," read the *Kansas City Star*. "Mrs. Larabee is a guest of Mr. and Mrs. Midgley."

LITTLE BY LITTLE, day by day, Ruth Larabee had been recovering. Her spirit may have been temporarily broken by the divorce, but over time her friends, her charity work, her travels, the chance to reconnect with family and the young Camp Fire Girls uplifted her. Undoubtedly the magic of her gardens and her precious quail also had a healing effect that contributed to her recuperation.

By 1952, Ruth was holding her head up high again in her trademark proud and resilient manner. In two photos with her friend Mary Carol Isaacs and the Camp Fire Girls, she is once again smiling and enjoying herself. The difference in her appearance from earlier photos when she was suffering from the divorce is striking.

ALSO DURING THESE post-divorce years, Ruth developed an attachment to the San Diego Natural History Museum. In late 1954 she wrote the following letter to the Museum's Board of Directors:

> Having been interested in the work of the Museum and in Wild Life conservation it is my wish to do something for your organization. I am therefore preparing

plans that upon my death I will give to the Society my ranch near Encinitas consisting of about 20 acres* on which I have placed various plants suitable to this climate."

Note: Since Ruth had given 4.2 acres to the Scouts, she now had a remainder of 22.3 acres of property remaining, not "20 acres" as she estimates in her letter.

She also intended to leave an endowment fund consisting of some of the real estate in Texas she had inherited from her father. She hoped the income from these properties would be adequate to maintain a portion of the ranch as a park for the Encinitas community "in perpetuity." With typical Ruth modesty, it was her wish that the gift would be anonymous and no publicity would mention her name. And she wanted the undeveloped portion of her land to remain undisturbed.

At first, the Museum officials were thrilled with the prospect, but as negotiations progressed they identified potential difficulties with the endowment and concluded that the property would be more useful to them if they had the option to eventually sell it and profit from the proceeds. This was, however, not what Ruth Larabee had in mind.

In the midst of her dealings with the Museum, it occurred to Ruth that she could make a direct gift of the residence property to San Diego County to be used as a park. This idea she let percolate for another few years, and in the meantime, she searched for other property to purchase for the Museum that would more appropriately suit their terms.

I<small>N</small> J<small>ULY</small> 1956, Ruth picked up her pen once more, this time to write a brief but life changing letter. The correspondence was directed to someone named "Mr. Howell," who was probably involved with the San Diego County Department of Parks and Recreation. Her writing was concise and to the point, or "no-nonsense" in classic Ruth Larabee style:

> I have lived in Encinitas for 14 years and observed the usefulness to this community of Glen Park in Cardiff. I have a 20 acre ranch just south of Mr. Ecke which I should like to will to the County for park use in the event of my death. I realize that it might not be acceptable. Will you please let me know how I may go about fulfilling this wish? I should be very glad to have the proper authorities make an inspection as soon as convenient … I am, yours sincerely, Ruth B. Larabee."

Her letter to the County marked a pivotal time in Ruth Larabee's life. She had reached the point where the occasional trips to Mexico didn't give her enough time to really accomplish her goals. She told friends that she planned to "go nurse to the poor," in whatever form that might take, and caring for the ranch was getting in the way. She had confronted her future, weighed her options, and decided to follow the calling in her heart.

Shortly after she penned this letter, Gerald Cullison, the Assistant Superintendent of Park Operation and Maintenance for San Diego County, called her and arranged a visit to the ranch. "She had a nice fire in the fireplace," he recalled, "and she was sitting in a rocking chair with a blanket over her lap. She was not too outgoing, but a very sensible person, the type of person who might be running a business."[66]

Over the course of the many meetings that followed, Cullison gained Ruth's trust and they developed a mutual level of respect. "Ruth had a lot of character. Some people like Ruth Larabee just impress you. You meet them and you are impressed because they are knowledgeable and reasonable," he said with admiration. By the time all was said and done, Cullison was able to convince her to donate the land sooner rather than later as a part of her will.

But Ruth had some caveats. She had become well acquainted with Cullison throughout the proceedings and stipulated that he must live at the ranch as the property administrator in order for the deal to go through. She told him, "I understand that this will be a lot of work. I would just like to feel that whoever I am turning this property over to will carry out my wishes." She needed reassurance that the ranch and the quail would be well cared for after she was gone and that the portion of the ranch which included the Del Mar manzanita and Southern maritime chaparral was protected for that purpose. She also wanted the property named "Quail Park" to protect what was for her one of its most important assets.

This threw Cullison a curve that he hadn't expected. "Now wait a minute," he said to the San Diego Board of Supervisors, "I can't do that. The house is just too small for me."

The Board immediately approved additions to the house which enlarged it on the north side. "After that, if I had refused the whole deal, the transfer would have fallen through," Cullison said. "I did not intend to live there in order to achieve this wonderful acquisition, but if I hadn't I would have been letting people down."

One of the deeds was transferred to the County in December 1956, and the second in January 1957, with a lease agreement allowing Ruth to stay another eight years if she wished. At that time, her property was valued at $98,000. However, in July 1957 she abruptly signed the papers that severed all ties, packed most of her belongings into the barn, and left El Rancho San Ysidro de las Flores for good.[67]

What compelled Ruth Larabee to leave the ranch in such haste and with such finality? Once she was gone, she scarcely looked back, almost as if she had had no choice but to flee from the memories. "The property was a part of her life she wanted to leave," Gerald Cullison observed. Was she driven to start life over in a completely different direction, to surrender the attachments that had to do with that chapter of her life? Did the heartbreak and sorrow surrounding her shattered marriage overshadow the richness and wonder she experienced in Encinitas? Or was it simply that without her gardening partner, Charles, the excitement of plants and gardens faded? Again, these are questions that may never be answered.

Not long after Ruth left, Gerald and Shirley Cullison married and held their wedding reception in the Walled Garden. Their son was born while they lived at the Larabee House, and Ruth sent him a Treasury Note for $25.

"I didn't see Ruth again for quite a while," Cullison said. "But then she happened to be visiting the park one day. She was sitting in the back seat of someone's car as they drove through. I saw her waving, but I recall that the man who was driving didn't stop."

Left: Harry and Jean Schneider with their daughter, Esther, in 1952, in Encinitas, California.

Below: Jean Schneider presents the Japanese doll and baby chair given to her by Ruth Larabee to San Diego Botanic Garden, March, 2016.

The Camp Fire Girls on the sandstone bluff outside Ruth's house, c1952. Ruth Larabee stands at the left, and Mary Carol Isaacs stands third from the right. Ruth Larabees' two dogs can be seen in the front row.

Retouched photo of Ruth Larabee extracted from the
Camp Fire Girls photo, c1952. This portrait hangs
in the Larabee House.

A Camp Fire Girls ceremonial event at the ranch, in February 1953.
This is possibly where the Kumeyaay demonstration home site is located today.
Ruth is in traditional costume standing far right, Mary Carol Isaacs
is third from the right, and Kathy Isaacs third from left.

Letter from Ruth Larabee to County officials, 1956.
Note that whereas she describes the ranch as containing "20 acres,"
the actual size at that time was 22.3 acres.

Looking eastward down the road from the Larabee House,
the row of Monterey cypress trees is still standing in the early 1960s.

Blooming foxtail agaves, Agave attenuata, *with the Larabee House barely visible in the background, in 1962.*

In 1964, an abundance of aloes, euphorbias and other succulents flourished downhill from the Larabee House not long after Ruth Larabee left.

CHAPTER 11

A COWBOY'S ADIÓS

You make all kinds of mistakes, but as long as you are generous and true
and also fierce, you cannot hurt the world or even seriously distress her.

—WINSTON S. CHURCHILL

What the next generation will value most is not what we owned,
but the evidence of who we were and the tales of how we lived.
In the end, it's the family stories that are worth storage.

—ELLEN GOODMAN, AMERICAN JOURNALIST

In 1954 Charles and Lila Larabee left Balboa Island and moved to a large home in Palm Desert, California, one of only a few built at the foot of Shadow Mountain. Charles did return to the ranch in Encinitas in 1962 and was given a tour by P.J. Miller, the County employee working as gardener and caretaker. After that, very little is known about Charles' life except that he managed the Larabee Family Trust until February 7, 1968 when he succumbed to lung cancer. He was 66 years old.

Charles' name can be seen on a crypt in the Larabee Family Mausoleum in Stafford, Kansas. However in reality his stepchildren Bill and Jean took his ashes from the crypt, and—together with those of their mother Lila, who passed away in 1988—delivered them to the desert wind and sky from the top of Shadow Mountain.

Charles Larabee's contributions were many. He was an avid, lifelong member of the Encinitas Rotary Club and supported countless good causes, including financing the college educations of more than a dozen young underprivileged students. Through his photography, he demonstrated a reverence for Latin cultures and the American Southwest and its heroes, documenting and preserving a portion of Americana which would be lost but for those like him who saw something worth saving. He was determined to share the grandeur of those places with as many people as possible on his guided river trips. And by daring to take on the ranch in Encinitas, he helped Ruth pave the way for what later became San Diego Botanic Garden.

Charles was a charitable person, and the instances on record are likely just a fraction of his lifetime of philanthropic activities. He had a generous spirit and a zest for life that was contagious. He was an optimist, and yes, he was the sort of person one just couldn't help but like.

But Charles Larabee's greatest gift—the one for which he will probably be most remembered—was the example he set for the Scouts and the young men he took under his wing. He was truly beloved by the next generations. He introduced them to the wonders of the natural world. He gave of himself with unbridled enthusiasm, and his concern for the wellbeing and education of others reflected the true measure of the man.

Charles Wright Larabee, age 50,
in Palm Desert, California, 1951.

CHAPTER 12

AT THE HANDS OF THE ELEMENTS

Life's got to be lived, no matter how long or short.
You got to take what comes.

—NATALIE BABBITT, TUCK EVERLASTING

After Ruth left Encinitas, she did follow her heart and move to Mexico to take up nursing. She relocated to Puebla, a city in the highlands of south central Mexico, and learned that the Baptist missionary "Hospital Latino America-na" on Calle Sur needed her help. Some of the hospital's patients could offer a small contribution for their treatment, but most had no money and were given charitable services. It would be possible to view Ruth's dramatic retreat to Puebla almost as an act of atonement.

This was where Ruth received her training as a nurse. In the process of that training, in August 1960, she wrote to Dr. George Lindsay, the Director of the San Diego Natural History Museum, expressing regret at missing his recent visit to Mexico. (Lindsay was a renowned botanist who specialized in desert plants.) Ruth wrote, "I have 12 hour night duty on the third floor alone, where we attend pediatric cases and the newly operated. It is really a great strain for poor old me, physically and emotionally. For this reason I really try to sleep eight or nine hours in the day."

In 1961, Lindsay wrote to Gerald Cullison back in Encinitas, informing him that Ruth completed her training and went to a remote village in the state of Puebla, "to do what she can for the Indians." Those details are uncertain, but it is clear that Ruth firmly established herself in Puebla, making friends and putting the needs of others ahead of her own. Some of these friends she named in her will and trust, like Juan and Jorge Gaspar, both Puebla residents, to whom she bequeathed $10,000 each to complete their college educations. In addition, she left money for nursing student Florina Morina and for Dr. F.L. Meadows, who also practiced in Puebla.

Ruth continued to make time for reading, which was always one of her favorite pastimes. She was moved by the popular novel "The Bridge Over the River Kwai" by Pierre Boulle, which explored the plight of World War II British prisoners of war forced by the Imperial Japanese Army to build a bridge for the "Death Railway" in Burma.

Ultimately Ruth Larabee had evolved and came to represent a new image of women. She was self-sufficient. She did not rely on men for her happiness or her finances. She had come into her own wealth and decided what she wanted to do with it, and how. She championed young women's rights. Her own children were the young women Scouts, the patients that she tended, and even more so, the garden plants and her beloved quail.

But it was evident that Ruth missed her connection to the outdoors and all that it meant for her heart and soul. "The greatest satisfaction in my disordered life has come from my contact with Nature," she wrote to Dr. Lindsay. "That is why I feel so much admiration for the Museum's work in giving these satisfactions to people of all ages."

Ruth was referring in part to the nature study programs and youth camps run by Charles "Harbie" Harbison, who was the entomologist for the Museum. She befriended Harbison when their paths crossed in her role as summer day camp director for San Dieguito. Harbison was known for bringing delight to children of all ages when he shared with them his classic museum trays full of insects of every type. Ruth valued the nature connections he made for young people and left a monetary gift in her will for him in support of his efforts. She herself had learned the language of nature, and recognized quite clearly that nature is a force of good.

Even from such a long distance, Ruth continued to search for the perfect property to give to the Museum and finally located three parcels to the south of San Marcos Drive (which is now Encinitas Boulevard.) "Before the end of the year I hope you will work out ... a method of accepting the parcels of land which I expressly bought for the Museum," she wrote Lindsay, "this time under your terms. Probably it will be more useful for your purpose to sell it and use the value in your own way, rather than to preserve a patch of chaparral."

Those three properties totaled 19 acres and were eventually deeded to the Museum with the hope that the land would increase in value and provide a good investment. They comprised land which is roughly bordered by today's streets named Encinitas Boulevard, Westlake Boulevard, Calle Magdalena, and Requeza Street, all of which was later sold largely for commercial use. In response to her gifts, the Museum made Ruth

Larabee a long distance honorary Patron.

Their relationship with Ruth didn't stop there. Knowing how much she still cared about the preservation of quail on her former ranch, they also stepped in to help foster the survival of her favorite little birds. Lindsay took it upon himself to make connections with the California Department of Fish and Game who had initiated a program in the 1950s to provide a self-sustaining water source to help improve quail habitat.

The Department adopted a unique watering system known as the "Gladding Gallinaceous Guzzler," named after its inventor. A sloping concrete apron channels water into sub-terranean storage tanks capable of holding about 1,000 gallons. Atop the tanks a small roof is built with steel bars to prevent larger animals from access. When the quail became hot and thirsty, they can walk into the cool shade of the man-made cave and get a much needed drink of water. Over 2000 of these guzzlers were installed in California with over 320 in San Diego County.[68] The guzzler at San Diego Botanic Garden is located in the Overlook Natural Area.

Lindsay personally oversaw the completion of the guzzler on Ruth's behalf. In the spring of 1962, he wrote her to say, "One of our best Nature Walks was to Quail Park, which is enjoying increasing use all of the time. The quail guzzler which you sponsored is full and ready for the birds this summer."

SOMETIME IN 1963, Ruth left Puebla and travelled in Spain and parts of Europe in the company of her sister Mary. When she finally returned to the United States, her new address was in Lubbock, Texas. For some reason, Ruth was drawn to this city in the northwestern part of the state, perhaps because Mary lived there. It was also the home of her step-mother

Katherine Adams Baird, Charles Baird's second wife.

She also developed a fondness for Texas Tech University in Lubbock and felt compelled to follow the model her father had set years before at the University of Michigan. She earmarked money in her will for the University to purchase a carillon for the west tower of the Administration Building, dedicated in memory of her parents, Charles and Georgia Baird.

In a huge gesture of support, Ruth and her sister endowed in their wills a total of 60 tracts of Texas real estate—inherited from their father Charles Baird—to Texas Tech. This land had surface value for the University at the time of sale and decades later the mineral rights generated enormous oil profits. Combining her attachment to the University and her belief in the value of training nurses, Ruth also made plans for the development of a nursing school at Texas Tech if there were proceeds remaining from her estate.

RUTH'S LAST KNOWN address was 5219 West 66th Street, in Shawnee Mission, a subdivision in Kansas City, Kansas. She had a charming little cottage surrounded by flowers, and she lived in a community where she was loved and had dear friends like Ingaborg Midgley. She had returned to her hometown around 1965 because it was comfortable and familiar, and she created a base camp from which she could continue to travel and visit friends and family. Ingaborg's daughter Nelani Midgley Walker remembered seeing Ruth during this period, and remarked about her kindness:

> Ruth called my mother to go out to dinner one evening. We went to pick her up and I happened to notice

a stunning, hand-appliqued quilt on her bed. 'That's a truly gorgeous quilt,' I commented, and Ruth said, 'It's yours,' and gave it to me on the spot. She was just such a generous person.'"

Ruth maintained contact with San Diegan Caroline Isaacs, who flew from California to visit her in Kansas City in 1968. Caroline recalls that "Ruth stayed busy gardening even while I was there. Her yard looked immaculate and didn't appear to need work, but she was so ardent about her flowers she just couldn't stay away from them."

Ruth continued to enjoy travel to destinations in Canada, the Bahamas, and Great Britain, although she was genuinely happy to return to Kansas City after each trip. "She was always telling me about how nice and well-educated the people were there," Caroline comments.

Then in the winter of 1969 Ruth Larabee's travels abruptly came to an end. She was on a pleasure trip that began in South Africa and continued to England, where she stayed at the "Rose and Crown," a medieval hotel in Saffron, Waldon just south of Cambridge. On December 26, a devastating fire started in the kitchen at 1:47 a.m. and ripped through the hotel. Seventy-five firefighters from ten brigades battled the blaze to rescue the hotel's 40 guests.

"People were hanging out of the windows yelling for help before the clouds of smoke reached them," one newspaper claimed.[69] But sadly, despite all efforts, eleven of the hotel guests perished from smoke inhalation. One of them was Ruth Baird Larabee. She was 65 years old and died two years after Charles passed away and just over two months before Quail Park Botanic Gardens opened to the public.

The disaster overseas was a sensation back in America that holiday season. News of the tragedy and of "the heiress" Ruth Larabee's demise was chronicled in papers from coast to coast. The cause of the blaze was significant enough to precipitate new safety legislation in England for every type of business. All of which was too late for Ruth Larabee.

"I feel quite sure I shall come to a watery grave."
—RUTH BAIRD ROBERTSON, AGE 16, IN 1920

The irony surrounding Ruth's tragic death is undeniable. Her auspicious beginning led to a most unfortunate end. The woman who as a young writer feared "a watery grave" perished instead at the hands of an entirely different foe, another of the four classic elements the ancient Greeks believed were the foundations of everything in existence. In the end she was taken by fire.

*Ruth Larabee as a registered nurse in 1961,
in Puebla, Mexico. This may have been her passport photo.*

A family gathering in Bloomfield Hills, Michigan, Christmas 1962.
Left to right: Ruth Larabee (age 58), her brother-in-law Marcus Eddy
Cunningham, Sr., her sister, Mary Baird Cunningham,
and their daughter, Susan Cunningham Williams.
Ruth's great-niece and nephew regarded her as "exotic" due to her deep tan,
brightly colored dress, and turquoise jewelry.

Caroline Isaacs with Ruth Larabee in front of her
lush garden in Kansas City in 1968. This was shortly before her death.

CHAPTER 13

A LIFE OF GENEROSITY

"Goodbye," said the fox.
"And now here is my secret,
a very simple secret:
It is only with the heart that one can see rightly;
what is essential is invisible to the eye."

—ANTOINE DE SAINT-EXUPÉRY, THE LITTLE PRINCE

Ruth's Larabee's remains were cremated in England and returned to Kansas City where she was buried near her parents at Forest Hill Cemetery. She had hoped her body could be returned to the Department of Anatomy, School of Medicine, University of Missouri, in Columbia for educational and scientific purposes, but that was not meant to be.

To honor their former student, The Barstow School made plans to create a memorial garden by transplanting to their grounds some of the special dwarf conifers Ruth had in her garden in Kansas City. Unfortunately, however, this did not come to pass.

With almost eerie foresight, Ruth wrote her will and trust just a few years before her death, painstakingly outlining bequests that would continue the good works she initiated during her lifetime. Among other things in her will, she bequeathed $10,000 to the San Diego Camp Fire Girls organization to provide assistance for young women in procuring uniforms, supplies and equipment. The scholarship fund Ruth Larabee initiated is still active today and has also been instrumental over the years in assisting qualified girls with their camping fees and Counselor in Training programs.

In her trust she named 70 beneficiaries, 55 of whom were non-family members, people who had been her friends and loved ones from all over the country and around the world. Her gifts to Texas Tech University keep on giving. Nearly fifty years after her death, their file containing Ruth's trust and probate records is still active as the various tracts of land she donated to them are leased for oil production. She also left an endowment to Tuskegee University in Alabama for scholarships for African American women.

But Ruth Baird Larabee's real legacy extends far beyond anything written in those documents. In her modest and understated way, she "paid it forward" to untold thousands of people. She cared deeply about the diversity of the natural world, was a role model for conservation and good stewardship, and sowed the seeds of wonder for countless generations to come. She gave her heart to younger generations and her land to the public, making it possible for San Diego Botanic Garden to exist today. Surely she would have been pleased with the result.

*Ruth Larabee was buried in the Baird family plot
at Forest Hill Cemetery in Kansas City.*

EPILOGUE
A DREAM BECOMES REALITY

"If you don't go after what you want, you'll never have it.
If you don't ask, the answer is always no. If you don't step forward,
you're always in the same place."

—NORA ROBERTS, AUTHOR

Thirteen years after Ruth Larabee gave her land to San Diego County, the park formally opened its gates to the public, fulfilling Ruth's wish. But when the gates did open in 1970, it was to "Quail Botanic Gardens" that people flocked. How and why did her 22.3 acres transition from a park to a full scale botanic garden?

The question of how the property transitioned was answered in part by Julia von Preissig, founding member and President of the Quail Gardens Foundation, Inc., in her May 1973 article for publication in the *Oceanside Blade Tribune*:

In 1957, Ruth Baird Larabee donated her estate in Encinitas to the County of San Diego, and a dream was born—to have a beautiful botanic garden for the benefit of everyone.

Little by little, this dream is taking on the form of reality through the cooperative efforts of the dedicated volunteers who form Quail Gardens Foundation, Inc., and the staffs of the County Parks and Recreation Department and the Park Development Division, with support of friends and the general public.

In the space of an article, how can the efforts and gifts of countless volunteers be recorded? Individuals and organizations, lay people and professionals, have poured time, skills and resources into the creation of a lovely, rustic garden with educational and scientific values.

This has been a step-by-step process to build a sound and enduring structure to develop gardens worthy of our area, so favored for the luxuriant growth of plants and flowers. Before any action was taken, outstanding people with such general assets as knowledge of growing conditions in the particular area, experience with other botanic gardens, skills in organization, etc., were called together. They agreed that this would be an excellent location for a botanic garden. With a long-range view and great attention to detail, the Foundation drew up by-laws, became incorporated in the State of California in 1961 and entered into a formal agreement with the County of San Diego.

In the early years, the planting progressed slowly while the County converted the private estate for public purposes, installing primary major necessities such as roads, parking lot, major water lines, and rest rooms.

Now that the groundwork has been laid, efforts can be concentrated upon adding to the trees, plants and flowers. The painstaking studies and planning are showing up in rare and lovely blooms, in bright and colorful vistas, in tree-shaded walks and fragrant nooks. The native quail, hidden at noonday in the chaparral with other wildlings, come out at dusk to feed. Groups of adults and children are led through the Gardens on guided tours. Camera and painting and nature study classes are conducted here. Visitors from every state in the union and from foreign countries come to wander and enjoy the Gardens.

The educational and scientific functions of a botanic garden are being developed through such means as labeling specimens, maintaining an herbarium of plants native to the premises, systematizing plant records and exchanging information and seeds with other botanic gardens. A botanic library is maintained for direct use for the Gardens. Records are maintained on agricultural and horticultural methods.

The Foundation spreads information about the Gardens through its own publications and those of others; through free slide programs for groups; through displays at public affairs and through person-to-person contacts.

To understand the present and to make plans for the future, it is helpful to look back to the past. To Gerald B. Cullison, now County Superintendent of Beaches and Parks, goes the credit for having proposed to Mrs. Larabee the idea of contributing her estate to the County and for having proposed that it be used as a botanic garden. Mrs. Larabee stipulated that her gift be used for the benefit of the public and asked that the quail be fed and that the place be named after the quail. Not only was the place officially named at that time Quail Park Botanic Gardens, but through the generous action of area residents, the street upon which it fronts was changed from Amersfoort Road to Quail Gardens Drive.

In the spring of 1959, Cletus Gardner, then Director of Parks and Recreation for the County, acquiesced to a proposal made by Julia von Preissig of Vista, that a volunteer group be formed to establish and help develop a botanic garden on the Larabee property. Dale T. Wood of Encinitas and Vista carried the idea to Dorothy Behrends of Encinitas, who in turn elicited enthusiastic response from garden clubs and plant societies.

Soon afterward, an informal meeting of garden-minded and knowledgeable people was held on the front porch of the dwelling on the premises. The hat was passed for contributions, and what was to become Quail Gardens Foundation, Inc., was launched. Of this original group that met fourteen years ago, remaining on the Board of Trustees are Bertha Benson of Pacific Beach, Paul Ecke of Encinitas, Onnolee Gould of La Jolla, Nelson Westree of Carlsbad and Julia von Preissig, now of San Diego. Of this original group, still interested and helpful are Dorothy Behrends, Horace Anderson of Encinitas, Esther Nesbin of San Marcos and Dale T. Wood of Vista. Joining shortly afterward were Mildred Macpherson of Encinitas, Foundation Landscape Chairman, and Florence Seibert of Escondido who served as President of the Foundation for the first six years. The list of volunteers who have contributed time, effort and resources for the Gardens would sound like a volume of Who's Who in the plant world of San Diego County."

Nelson E. Westree, mentioned above, was another professional who connected the Larabee's former estate with larger developments in San Diego history. A longtime member of the Foundation Board, he was the first Superintendent of the Carlsbad Parks Department and an authority on trees, especially fruit and nut trees.

Westree advised actor Leo Carrillo on plantings and on his extensive citrus orchard at Carrillo's Carlsbad property, "Rancho de los Kiotes," which Carrillo purchased in 1937. Carrillo was interested in planting avocados and other more unusual Latin American fruit trees on his ranch. (A portion of the ranch is open to the public as the Leo Carrillo Ranch Historic Park.)

Today Leo Carrillo is best remembered for his role as "Pancho" in the 1950s television show, "The Cisco Kid." But he was also actively involved for many years through the California Beaches and Parks Commission in conservation and historic preservation of sites around the state, including Anza-Borrego Desert State Park and Hearst Castle.

As a founding board member of the new botanic garden, Westree advocated an orchard of various subtropical fruit trees to replace the aging avocado grove on the west side of the Garden. In the early 1970s the subtropical fruit garden was planted, as explained below in the continuation of Julia von Preissig's remarks:

> Over the period of time, a number of members of County staff have been actively involved in the development of the Gardens. Head Gardener P.J. Miller and Mrs. Miller and his assistant, Clarence Heidemann and Mrs. Heidemann have been long-time residents on the property and have taken special interest in the care and growth of the Gardens.
>
> Since the outset, there have been many changes. The original estate of Ruth Larabee had been laid out primarily as a home site and commercial avocado grove. For a time after the take-over by the County, this plot served as a study area for the U.C. Riverside Experiment Station in the effect of Bermuda grass in an avocado grove. As many of the trees went into decline, they were removed and the area was leveled and prepared for the planting of a grove of subtropical fruit

trees by the Foundation, now started and planned to be one of the outstanding features of the Gardens.

Members and friends of the Foundation have donated funds and rare plants for addition to the already outstanding planting of cactus and other succulents, and have contributed funds and other gifts in the form of approved trees, shrubs and flowering plants. Restful benches and bird watering basins have been contributed by clubs. The Foundation has donated a glasshouse fort the germination of seeds and the propagation of cuttings. Soon to be erected is a shade house for the care of seedlings and protection of new plants awaiting placement in the Gardens. This will be the culmination of a project finance long ago as a memorial.

A notable planting of proteas has served as inspiration for the start of many such in home gardens. A bromeliad plot is being expanded in a favorable location where these exotic plants are naturalizing.

Currently, the Gardens are being equipped with a very advanced type of automatic watering system, the very generous gift of Wm. B. Crane whose Plantmation Company is headquartered in Solana Beach, and E.J. Hunter of the Moist O'Matic Division of Toro Company of Riverside, who is soon to make his home in the North County of San Diego.

Dreams for the future of the Gardens include full development of the entire acreage with the exception of the five acres reserved in native chaparral. Envisioned is a major shade house for special plant displays and permanent plantings of rare and exotic plants; a gazebo to offer a gracious resting spot among the subtropical fruit trees; the development of a nature trail and outdoor amphitheater; an bird watching station; furnishings and equipment of the Foundation headquarters and activities building; more and more plant labels and explanatory signs and a full program of classes, workshops and special events."

Note: The Quail Gardens Foundation that von Preissig mentions, (before it became Quail Gardens Foundation, Inc.) was composed of the following people: Officers: President, Mrs. M.J. von Preissig, First Vice President, Mrs. R.C. Lawton, Second Vice President, Mrs. Mildred Macpherson, Treasurer, Paul V. Lane, and Secretary, Mrs. Edwin Gould. Honorary Directors: Chauncey I. Jerabek, Dr. G. E. Lindsay, and Mrs. Ruth Larabee. Directors: Mrs. Paul W. Behrends, Mrs. Clarence W. Benson, Dr. Ernest E. Dale, Mr. Paul Ecke, Mrs. Ralph Goldsmith, Mrs. Esther Nesbin, Dr. Ralph S. Roberts, James Saracino, Mrs. A.R. Seibert, Walter Watchorn, Nelson E. Westree, and Dale T. Wood.

JULIA VON PREISSIG'S summary does not fully explain why the property evolved into a full-scale botanic garden rather than being limited to a park for the conservation of quail, as Ruth Larabee requested. The aforementioned Dale T. Wood explained the thinking behind this evolution in 1964 in the first

Quail Call, the newsletter of the Quail Gardens Foundation, Inc. His article entitled, "A Gift and a Puzzle," read as follows:

> Part of the [22.3-acre] ranch home of Ruth Larabee had become the showplace for her remarkable collection of plants. Few of them were common. Some were downright rare. This was particularly true of her remarkable collection of cacti and succulents.
>
> A rugged area including bluff and ravine had been left in picturesque naturalness of chaparral. Mrs. Larabee's interest in this remarkable natural collection was well placed as over 70 species of local native plants grow here. It also served an additional interest—enjoyment of the bird life. This native cover furnishes the principal habitat for a hundred or more California quail. Her enjoyment of them—they became almost pets— suggested the name for the park.
>
> To the west of the walled yard adjacent to Mrs. Larabee's residence was a small avocado grove. And the few remaining westerly acres are being farmed by "The Poinsettia King," Paul Ecke.
>
> Ruth Larabee's gift in 1957 was a demonstration of confidence and a high compliment to our County Park Commission and its executive officer Cletus Gardener, Director of Parks and Recreation, along with his whole staff. Such things do not occur in an atmosphere of mistrust or lack of enthusiasm.
> But now came the puzzle. How should the park be developed? ... Someone within the team of people as-

sembled by Julia von Preissig suggested that since the property already had the sizeable nucleus of a remarkable horticultural exhibit it might be well to devote the whole park to this type of development. The Santa Barbara Botanic Garden and the L.A. Arboretum were examples. … A horticultural park was unanimously approved.

With our growing population, Director Gardner was concerned with the future need for play space in the area. Would it not be practical to use a small plot at the west end of the property for playground development? In fact, as the demand grew, would the use of the entire park area for horticulture be politically tenable? This issue was settled at a meeting with the County Park Commission on March 1, 1961. Paul Ecke, one of those representing our Foundation, gave five acres of nearby land—now Ecke Field—for playground purposes. So the last item in the puzzle of policy was solved by this generous act."

IN 1961, DURING the time described by von Preissig and Wood, P. J. Miller (Pius John) was hired to lead the San Diego County Parks and Recreation staff. He was a World War II veteran who was present at the front on D-Day. During the war he met his British-born wife, Chris, at London's Royal Botanic Gardens at Kew.

After the war Miller worked in Southern California and was later hired by the County of San Diego to lead the development of the new garden in Encinitas. He supervised the County's extensive garden restoration and maintenance. He coordinated with contractors in building maintenance and the installation of roads, restrooms, water lines, irrigation, and a parking lot.

P.J. Miller liked flowering plants, from annuals and perennials to azaleas and camellias. He particularly favored having pockets of colorful garden plants in key visible locations throughout the Garden. Some of the oldest of these plants in the Garden today are ones that he planted decades ago.

Miller also enjoyed propagating plants, especially unusual species, like silver trees and dawn redwoods. He and his wife traveled to England several times and visited gardens, bringing back plants and seeds. Nursery friend Horace Anderson encouraged him to utilize a wide variety of unusual tropical and subtropical species.

Miller and his wife lived in the Lawn House until 1970 when they moved to the Larabee House. Bill Nelson, owner of Pacific Tree Farms nursery, remembered Miller as very energetic, saying, "If you wanted to talk to P.J. you had to talk on the run, as he went from one job to the next."

Clarence Heidemann joined the staff as a Gardener in 1964 and later lived with his wife, Bernie, in the Lawn House. Heidemann was a World War II Marine veteran who served in the Pacific, including the Midway Islands, and Iwo Jima. He retired from the Marines in 1961 as a Master Sargeant. Like Miller, Heidemann was dedicated and hard working.

THE COMPLETE ACCOUNT of hard work and dedication resulting in the opening of the Gardens and its early years could fill an entirely separate publication. Most importantly, as Julia von Preissig recorded in her article, the Foundation's efforts came to fruition on March 8, 1970—just months after Ruth Larabee passed away—when Quail Botanic Gardens formally opened to the public. As Foundation President, von Preissig addressed the gathered members, dignitaries and public at the formal opening with the following inspiring words:

> We dream and work toward preserving the rustic charm of the estate, its fine, old plantings and its natural life; toward endowing the gardens with the choicest trees, shrubs, and flowers; toward cultivating a center for research and study; and toward developing all those features which will provide a quiet haven for the delight of people, young and old, from near and far."

*Left to right: P.J. Miller, Quail Botanic Gardens foreman,
along with Mildred Macpherson and Nelson Westree,
Directors of Quail Gardens Foundation, Inc.,
review the drawings for a new planting area, 1967.*

*Foundation President Julia von Preissig
admires bromeliads at Quail Botanic Gardens,
which was established thanks to her dedication
and commitment. Photo c1970.*

AFTERWORD

—DAVE EHRLINGER, DIRECTOR OF HORTICULTURE
SAN DIEGO BOTANIC GARDEN, 2002 TO 2013

Since its official formal opening in 1970 as a partnership between San Diego County and the Quail Gardens Foundation, Inc., the Garden has seen significant development and transformation from a small county park to a nationally recognized botanic garden. Some of this was described by Julia von Preissig, and in fact there were hundreds of steps along the way and countless inspiring people like von Preissig who made this transformation possible.

IT BEGAN WITH some good news from Paul Ecke, Sr., one of the Foundation's original Board members, who donated the 4.2-acre property south of the Garden to the County as an addition in 1971. The building on that property, initially known as the Scout Hut, became invaluable as the activity and administrative center of the Garden. Three years later the building was remodeled and renamed the Ecke Family Building

Unfortunately, two of the most important leaders of the Garden passed away within a few months of each other in 1973. One of those was Julia von Preissig herself, the President of the Quail Gardens Foundation, Inc., and Chair of the Liaison Committee who had worked tirelessly for years with the County and numerous other organizations to ensure success for the Garden. County administrator Gerald Cullison remembered Julia von Preissig as "a strong lady, an organizer, who carried the ball."

The second loss was Mildred Macpherson, the certified landscape architect who as previously mentioned co-owned the Williams-Macpherson Nursery in Encinitas where Ruth Larabee bought many unusual plants over the years. Macpherson was Chairman of the Foundation's Landscape Committee during the formative years of the 1960s. She was also an educator, serving as a teacher, dean and principal of schools in Encinitas. She was on the San Diego County Board of Education for 24 years. A close friend of Paul Ecke, Sr. and his wife Magdalena, Macpherson worked with County staff as the Foundation's representative in planning garden restorations and future projects. When she died she left a bequest to install a dramatic waterfall (later named in her honor) at the head of the canyon that is now the Tropical Rain Forest.

After these losses in leadership, Florence Seibert, who had been the Foundation's first President in 1964, stepped in and became the President pro tem for eighteen months. H. S. Sherman, Julia von Preissig's brother, capably served as President for the next four years. Eventually a group of younger leaders with new energy and enthusiasm got involved in the Garden, including Archibald "Archie" Owen, Bill Gunther, and Richard Haubrich.

In 1974 they were joined by Gil Voss, a knowledgeable botanist and zoologist who graduated from San Diego State University.

Before long, large plant sales staffed by Foundation volunteers were held at the Garden to raise funds, with plants donated by local nurseries and many plant societies. Christmas holiday events also became popular.

East of the Ecke Family Building the original Southern maritime chaparral and its rare Del Mar manzanitas were preserved through the efforts of noted botanist Mitchel ("Mitch") Beauchamp, President of the young San Diego Native Plant Society. In a letter to the County he noted the chaparral's value to the quail and other wildlife. He also recommended installing paths in these areas along which plants could be labeled and identified for visitors.

The major project for the late 1970s was the installation of the Mildred Macpherson Waterfall. After extensive planning between the County and the Foundation the spectacular project was dedicated on March 11, 1979. Designed and built by Torzeski Studios, the complex installation required a crane to set huge boulders in place in a naturalistic fashion. Gardener Gil Voss acquired plants from a wide variety of nursery sources and was in charge of landscaping.

In 1978 P.J. Miller retired. Gil Voss was later appointed Horticulturist and he and his wife, Alison, moved into the Larabee House. Voss brought a more scientific, museum-like approach to botanical garden operations. He organized the Garden into geographic areas, an organizational pattern that was common at the time, especially in California botanical gardens. For years he went on regular collecting trips to Central Mexico, focusing on the ethnobotany of the Huichol Indians.

Alison Voss supported her husband in a variety of Garden activities and organized the Docent Society in 1981 to train more volunteers to support the Garden by providing tours, and staffing the nursery, herbarium, library, and various events. County Gardener Steve Brigham supervised the construction of new nursery facilities, improved nursery operations, and expanded plant collections.

The American Bamboo Society was started at the Garden in 1979. Among its founders were Gil Voss, Quail Gardens Foundation, Inc., Board member Richard Haubrich, and Bill Teague, later a Garden staff member. The Garden's collection of bamboo, which began in the late 1970s, has long been the largest collection in any U.S. public garden.

In 1982 landscape architect Paul Mahalik designed a landscape in memory of the founding Garden Board Member, nurseryman Horace Anderson. As an extension of Palm Canyon this garden simulated the tropical foothills of the Himalayas using fishtail palms, *Caryota urens* and other appropriate species. Mahalik later designed an addition to the Waterfall, which was built in 1986. This created a stream from the Waterfall pond that apparently ran under the walkway and through the tropical forest down to a lower pond. Although appearing to be connected with the Waterfall, it is actually a separate water feature. This landscape addition was artfully crafted and remains very popular with visitors today.

In 1985 a land swap was made between the County and a local development company. Property along Saxony Road on the west side of the Garden was traded for land previously owned by Hans Hartman. This included three houses and what is now another parking lot. The Silverado Encinitas Memory Care Community facility was later built on the Saxony Road site.

In 1986 the Visitor Center and Gift Shop were built, expanding visitor services. In addition to plant sales the Garden hosted weddings, concerts, arts and crafts fairs, and flower and plant shows.

In 1988 the County appointed Steve Hendrix as Superintendent. He resided in the largest of the three Hartman houses north of the Subtropical Fruit Garden near the Ecke Ranch.

The Garden received a federal Institute of Museum Services (I.M.S.) grant in 1988 to inventory, tag, and map the Garden's collections of bamboos, cycads, and palms. The plant records system was computerized, and the Garden was surveyed. Grid markers were installed to aid in mapping the Garden's plant collection.

In the early 1990s students at Mira Costa College developed a special garden in the northeast corner of the Garden along Quail Gardens Drive to demonstrate the merits of California native plants.

The Overlook Tower opened in 1992. Its wooden boardwalk was built to protect the sensitive Southern maritime chaparral habitat in which it is located. A few weeks later the gazebo in the Lawn Garden was dedicated and became an enormously popular garden feature, especially as a backdrop for weddings.

In the late 1980s San Diego County had serious financial problems and the Parks and Recreation Department was forced to make cutbacks. Ultimately, in 1993, San Diego County tax support for the Garden was terminated. The Quail

Gardens Foundation, Inc., negotiated a lease with the County in which the Foundation would manage and operate the Garden for five years, from Oct. 28, 1993 to Oct. 27, 1998, while the County retained ownership. From this point on the Garden was financially supported by admissions, membership, gift shop and plant sales, donations, and a variety of fund-raising activities.

The Insect Fair began in the early 1990s. With its small, kid-sized creatures it has always been a popular and educational event for children and their families. Summer concerts were also held in the Garden.

Through the difficulties of this period, in view of the loss of County revenues, a core group of Board members, docents, volunteers, and supportive people from both local and extended communities were critical to the Garden's support. Joyce Wilder was Board President from 1994 to 1996. In 1994 the Ecke Family Building was remodeled to improve its use as the Garden's administrative and education center. A search was conducted to hire an executive director in 1994. In January 1995 Julian Duval began his long tenure. In the same year the Canary Islands Garden was opened.

The Garden of Lights began in 1996 as an evening event during the winter holiday season. Thousands of holiday lights are hung to create delightful nighttime charm. Features include carolers, roasting marshmallows, crafts for kids, horse drawn wagon rides, and a visit with Santa.

A series of garden improvements took place in the late 1990s. The Bamboo Garden opened in 1996 with new plantings, pathways, irrigation, and signs. A pond was installed which was soon popular, with small fish, bullfrogs, turtles, and water lilies. A sculpture entitled "Asian Shadows," by noted local sculptor and architect James Hubbell, was installed by the pond. In 1996 docent Nils Lunnerdal installed the "Landscape for Fire Safety" garden to protect the Ecke Family Building from wildfires as well as to demonstrate appropriate landscape design and fire-resistant plants.

In 1997 the Subtropical Fruit Garden was upgraded with new plantings, pathways, signs, and irrigation. Plant identification and larger interpretive signs were installed to inform visitors about cultivating fruits in home gardens and landscapes. The following year the Waterfall area was enhanced with new plantings and signs. It was renamed the "Rain Forest" to focus on this biologically diverse area and its conservation concerns.

In 2000 the first annual "Gala" evening fund-raising event was held. This features food and beverages served in attractive garden locations, followed by an auction with a guest honoree. Each year the funds raised from this event contribute to a specific project or much needed equipment.

The Native Plants and Native People display opened in 2000 in the chaparral outside the Ecke Family Building. Educational signs point out plants and describe the ethnobotany of the Kumeyaay indigenous people who once lived in San Diego. A Kumeyaay ewaa dwelling and a ramada were constructed, along with a recirculating pond and stream.

During this period the Foundation Board of Trustees was strengthened under its President, Jim Farley, with improved governance policies, organization, and operations.

In 2003 the Seeds of Wonder Children's Garden opened as a trial garden for a larger future children's garden. Later in 2003 the Garden signed a 55-year lease with the city of Encinitas for the 4.5-acre property to the north which was once owned by the Ecke family. The San Dieguito Heritage Museum was given 1.2 acres of the site to install facilities in their mission of preserving and interpreting local history. In 2003 Quail Gardens Drive was extended north to Leucadia Drive, greatly increasing traffic flow past the Garden's entrance.

In the early years of the new century most of the Garden got a fresh, new look when large areas were renovated with new plantings, landscaping, irrigation, and signs, under Director of Horticulture Dave Ehrlinger, Horticulture Resource Specialist Bill Teague, Horticulture Manager Liz Rozycki, and Facilities Manager Sergio Bautisto.

Several new gardens were added, including the popular Undersea Succulent Garden, the Mexican Garden with its delightful topiaries, the South African Garden, and the Succulent Display Garden. With a new awareness of water conservation, both locally and statewide, most of these gardens featured succulents and other drought tolerant plants. Conservation and sustainability have been ongoing themes in all the Garden's operations.

Along with growing attendance during this period, all the functions of the Garden expanded from education and events to fundraising and membership. Operations Director Pat Hammer, Education and Events Manager Diana Goforth, and Development Director Tracie Barham provided leadership in these areas.

In 2009 the Hamilton Children's Garden opened, the largest project ever undertaken by the Garden. It was named after Board member Frances Hamilton White who pledged one million dollars for the construction as well as providing other Garden support. It greatly increased attendance and membership, appealing to the Millennial generation and their young children as well as to Baby Boomers and their grandchildren.

Its main feature is Toni's Tree House, situated atop a 25 foot artificial tree which towers over a dozen themed gardens and features, from Incredible Edibles to the Mountain Stream and Quail Haven, a display of the Garden's signature bird.

Later in the year the name of the Garden was changed from "Quail Botanical Gardens" to the "San Diego Botanic Garden," a sign of its changing regional focus and significance.

In 2012 the Visitor Center and Gift Shop and its nursery were enlarged and remodeled. The shops were renamed The Garden Shops. The Welcome Center was installed, improving admissions operations and traffic flow. Sculpture in the Garden began, featuring works by regional artists displayed in natural, picturesque settings.

In 2013 the Garden joined the Center for Plant Conservation, a national organization dedicated to conserving rare North American plants through a network of botanical gardens and arboreta. The Garden also joined the American Public Garden Association's Plant Collections Network with its bamboo collection.

As a measure of the Garden's growth, from the early 1980s to the year 2000, the annual attendance had plateaued at about 100,000 visitors per year. After 2000, attendance steadily rose until in 2015 it was over 230,000 visitors per year, while membership increased even more.

AS SAN DIEGO Botanic Garden looks to the future, the next major project is the development of the Dickinson Family Education Conservatory to be located north of the Hamilton Children's Garden. It will feature a conservatory of tropical plants amidst spaces for educational classes and events.

Garden horticulture and facility staff offices and storage will move from the Larabee House and the Lawn House to a new building constructed by the County. The Larabee House and the Lawn House will then serve a variety of public functions. The former will serve as a center for the story of the Garden's Larabee history, as well as a location for wedding personnel and meetings. Plans are in place to restore the front (east-facing) porch to more closely resemble its appearance when Ruth and Charles lived there. Some years after Ruth left, the porch was enclosed to create office space for the horticultural staff, and soon it will be returned to something similar to its original status.

Another plan for future growth arose as a result of the Leichtag Foundation's purchase in 2012 of the Paul Ecke Ranch property to the north. That property has been developed as an innovative model to connect people to their community, to demonstrate best practices for growing food, and the importance of the land and social justice based on historic Jewish practices. Thanks to the Leichtag Foundation, there are future plans to donate a number of acres of this property to San Diego Botanic Garden to expand the Garden with a new entry, parking, visitor center and conservatory.

SAN DIEGO BOTANIC Garden will continue to be a vital part of the growth and development of San Diego's North County community and greater San Diego in years to come. For example, the Garden has partnered with the local school district, the Leichtag Foundation, and other neighboring institutions, including the Magdalena Ecke YMCA, the San Dieguito Heritage Museum, and Seacrest Village Retirement Communities, to form the "Encinitas Environmental Education (E3) Cluster."

This project began in 2015 when the Encinitas Union School District opened an Agro-Ecology Learning Center across from SDBG on Quail Gardens Drive, which also features a local community garden. Growth of the E3 Cluster is based on a cooperative agreement made between all of the organizations, "...to develop educational, experiential learning and multigenerational programs around the nexus of agriculture, horticulture, science, sustainability, community building, and the local history and agricultural traditions of Encinitas."

APPENDICES

TODAY AT SAN DIEGO
BOTANIC GARDEN

The pages that follow offer a virtual tour of San Diego Botanic Garden 60 years after Ruth Larabee gave her land to the people of San Diego. Due to space limitations, this is but a fraction of the beauty and wonder that can be enjoyed in this garden oasis nearly every day of the year.

Above: Entrance to the Garden.
Below: Sign that greets visitors at the Seeds of Wonder Children's Garden.

*Outside the Walled Garden at the Larabee House
where Ruth Larabee sat in 1951.*

A dragon tree, Dracaena draco, *in the Old World Desert Garden. This is the logo tree for San Diego Botanic Garden.*

179

A male California quail at San Diego Botanic Garden.

The Mildred Macpherson Waterfall
flows into the Tropical Rainforest below.

Endangered Del Mar manzanita, Arctostaphylos glandulosa ssp. crassifolia, *preserved near the Overlook Natural Area.*

Above: Amazon water lily, Victoria amazonica, *in the Bamboo Garden.*
Below: Blue century plants, Agave americana, *in the Mexican Garden.*

"Toni's Tree House" and the Hamilton Children's Garden.

Pattern and texture in the Undersea Succulent Garden.

Decorative boulders line a dry creek bed in the Australian Garden.

Above: A dragonfly hovers over a water lily in the Bamboo Garden pond.
Below: This great horned owl is perched in a eucalyptus tree, Eucalyptus cladocalyx.

*Peeking at the Kids' Cottage
in the Seeds of Wonder Children's Garden.*

*An original sculpture enhances the space
in the Bamboo Garden.*

Exploring the Mountain Stream in the Hamilton Children's Garden.

Deep within the Tropical Rain Forest.

Above: Lotus blossoms are an annual sight in the Bamboo Garden pond.
Below: Dragon fruit, Hylocereus undatus, *in the Subtropical Fruit Garden.*

The artfully designed succulent topiary waitress in the Mexican Garden.

A green heron fishing in the Bamboo Garden pond.

A family moment in the Bamboo Garden.

Blooming elephant's foot trees, Beaucarnea recurvata,
frame the Undersea Succulent Garden.

View of the New World Desert Garden.

Water play in the Hamilton Children's Garden.

Bananas in the Subtropical Fruit Garden.

199

PLANT LIFE OF QUAIL PARK

AN INVENTORY OF PLANTS THAT WERE PRESENT IN 1962

—CHAUNCEY I. JERABEK, HONORARY DIRECTOR

QUAIL GARDENS FOUNDATION, INC.

Originally written for *California Garden*, June-July 1962.

AGAVES AND OTHER SUCCULENTS

Aeonium haworthii, Pinwheel Aeonium
Agave attenuata, Foxtail Agave
Agave angustifolia, Caribbean Agave
Agave victoriae-reginae, Queen Victoria Agave
Aloe arborescens, Candleabra Aloe
*Aloe barbarae (*formerly *A. bainesii),* Tree Aloe
Aloe cameronii, Red Aloe
Aloe distans, Jewel Aloe
Aloe ferox, Cape Aloe
Aloe humilis var. *echinata*
Aloe maculata (formerly *A. saponaria),* Soap Aloe
Aloe plicatilis, Fan Aloe
Aloe speciosa, Showy Aloe
Aloe x spinosissima
Aloe striata, Coral Aloe
Aloe succotrina
Aloe vera, Medicinal Aloe
Bromelia pinguin (formerly *B. fastuosa)*
Crassula multicava, Fairy Crassula
Cotyledon orbiculata, Pig's Ear
Crassula ovata (formerly *C. argentea),* Jade Plant
Dasylirion wheeleri, Sotol
Dracaena draco, Dragon Tree
Gasteria species, Gasteria
Kalanchoe beharensis, Felt Bush
Senecio serpens (formerly *Kleinia repens),* Blue Chalk-Sticks
Manfreda maculosa, Manfreda
Portulacaria afra, Elephant's Food
Puya alpestris, Sapphire Tower
Puya chilensis, Chilean Puya
Yucca carnerosana, Tree Yucca

CACTI

Cereus jamacaru
Cereus peruvianus, Peruvian Apple Cactus
Cereus peruvianus var. *monstrosus,* Monstrose Peruvian Apple Cactus
Cereus validus
Myrtillocactus geometrizens, Garambullo
Opuntia ficus-indica, Mission Prickly Pear
Pachycereus pringlei, **Cardon**
Stenocereus thurberi, Organ Pipe Cactus

EUPHORBIAS

Euphorbia canariensis, Canary Island Spurge
Euphorbia coerulescens
Euphorbia cooperi, Bushveld Candelabra Euphorbia
Euphorbia grandidens
Euphorbia ingens, Tree Euphorbia
Euphorbia mammillaris
Euphorbia pentagona
Euphorbia. pseudocactus
Euphorbia resinifera, Resin Spurge
Euphorbia tetragona, African Milk Tree

EUCALYPTUS

Corymbia citriodora (formerly *Eucalyptus citriodora),* Lemon-Scented Gum
Corymbia ficifolia (formerly *Eucalyptus ficifolia),* Red-Flowering Gum
Eucalyptus cladocalyx, Sugar Gum
Eucalyptus macrocarpa, Mottlecah
Eucalyptus rhodantha, Rose Mallee
*Eucalyptus camaldulensis (*formerly *Eucalyptus rostrata),* River Red Gum

MESEMBRYANTHEMUMS

Drosanthemum speciosum, Red Ice Plant
Glottiphyllum linguiforme

ACACIAS

Acacia baileyana, Bailey Acacia
Acacia cultriformis, Knife Acacia
Acacia decurrens, Green Wattle
Acacia linifolia, Flax-Leafed Wattle
Acacia pravissima, Oven's Wattle
Acacia retinodes, Swamp Wattle
Acacia verticillata, Prickly Moses

FRUIT TREES

Annona cherimola, Cherimoya, Custard Apple
Carissa grandiflora, Natal plum
Citrus x *meyeri*, Meyer Lemon
Citrus x *paradisi*, Grapefruit
Citrus reticulata, Tangerine
Citrus sinensis, Orange
Eriobotrya japonica, Loquat
Fortunella margarita, Kumquat
Macadamia integrifolia, Macadamia
Olea europaea, Olive
Prunus persica, Peach
Psidium guajava, Guava
Punica granatum, Pomegranate

OTHER TREES

Araucaria bidwillii, Bunya-Bunya
Araucaria heterophylla (formerly *A. excelsa)*, Star Pine, Norfolk Island Pine
Arbutus unedo, Strawberry Tree
Callistemon viminalis, Weeping Bottlebrush
Calodendrum capense, Cape Chestnut
Cercis canadensis, Eastern Redbud
Cinnamomum camphora, Camphor Tree
Cunninghamia lanceolata, China Fir
Cupressus macrocarpa, Monterey Cypress
Erythrina americana, Coral Tree
Erythrina caffra, South African Coral Tree
Ficus lutea, (formerly *F. utilis)* Zulu Fig
Ficus microcarpa (formerly *F. nitida)*, Indian Laurel Fig
Ficus mysorensis, Mysore Fig
Grevillea robusta, Silk Oak
Jacaranda mimosifolia (formerly *J. acutifolia)*, Jacaranda
Juniperus chinensis 'Torulosa,' Hollywood Juniper
Leucadendron argenteum, Silver Tree
Melaleuca armillaris, Drooping Melaleuca
Melia azedarach 'Umbraculiformis', Texas Umbrella Tree
Parkinsonia aculeata, Jerusalem Thorn
Pinus canariensis, Canary Island Pine
Pinus torreyana, Torrey Pine
Pistacia chinensis, Chinese Pistache
Podocarpus henkelii, Long-Leaved Yellowwood, Fern Pine
Podocarpus macrophyllus, Yew Pine
Pyrus kawakamii, Evergreen Pear
Quercus suber, Cork Oak
Sophora japonica, Pagoda Tree
Spathodea campanulata, African Tulip Tree

PALMS AND KINDRED PLANTS

Archontophoenix cunninghamiana, King Palm
Brahea armata, Mexican Blue Palm
Brahea edulis, Guadalupe Palm
Butia capitata, Pindo Palm, Jelly Palm
Ceratozamia species
Cussonia capensis, Cussonia
Howea forsteriana, Kentia Palm
Philodendron eichleri, King of the Tree Philodendron
Philodendron selloum
Phoenix roebelinii, Pygmy Palm
Strelitzia nicolai, Giant Bird of Paradise
Syagrus romanzoffianum, Queen Palm
Washingtonia filifera, California Fan Palm

SHRUBS

Abutilon megapotamicum, Flowering Maple
Abutilon speciosum, Flowering Maple
Anthyllis barba-jovis, Jupiter's Beard
Bauhinia galpinii, Red Bauhinia
Caesalpinia echinata, Brazil Wood
Caesalpinia gilliesii (formerly *Poinciana gilliesii*), Yellow Bird of Paradise
Calliandra haematocephala (formerly *C. aequilatera*), Pink Powder Puff
Carissa congesta (formerly *C. carandas*, Karanda
Cistus x *hybridus* (formerly *C. corbariensis*, White Rock Rose
Convolvulus cneorum, Bush Morning Glory
Duranta repens, Sky Flower or Golden Dew Drop
Elaeagnus pungens, Silverberry
Escallonia laevis (formerly *E. organensis*), Pink Escallonia
Grevillea lanigera, Wooly Grevillea

Grewia occidentalis, Lavender Starflower
Hibiscus rosa-sinensis, Tropical Hibiscus
Ilex aquifolium, English Holly
I. cornuta, Chinese Holly
I. cornuta 'Burford', Burford Chinese Holly
Leonotis leonurus, Lion's Tail
Ligustrum lucidum, Glossy Privet
Michelia figo (formerly *Michelia fuscata*), Banana Shrub
Myrsine africana, African Boxwood
Osteomeles anthyllidifolia, Uhi-Uhi
Pittosporum eugenioides, Tarata Pittosporum
Pittosporum tobira 'Variegata', Variegated Mock Orange
Plumbago capensis, Cape Plumbago
Pyracantha species, Firethorn
Rhaphiolepis umbellata (formerly *R. ovata*), Yeddo Hawthorn
Senna didymobotrya (formerly *Cassia nairobensis*), Popcorn Senna
Syringa vulgaris, Lilac
Syzygium paniculatum, Australian Brush Cherry
Tecoma capensis (formerly *Tecomeria capensis*), Cape Honeysuckle
Tecoma stans, Yellow Bells
Tibouchina urvilleana (formerly *T. semidecanduspensum*), Glory Bush
Viburnum suspensum, Sadankwa Viburnum

OTHER PLANTS

Acanthus mollis, Bear's Breech
Adiantum species, Maidenhair Fern
Amaryllis belladonna, Belladona Lily, Naked Lady
Arctotis acaulis, African Daisy
Cyperus haspan 'Viviparus', Miniature Umbrella Plant
Dietes iridioides (formerly *Moraea iridioides*), African Iris
Osteospermum ecklonis (formerly *Dimorphotheca ecklonis*), Cape Marigold
Distictis buccinatorius, Red Trumpet Vine
Echium fastuosum, Pride of Madeira

Felicia amelloides, Blue Marguerite
Ficus pumila, Creeping Fig
Fuchsia hybrid, Fuchsia
Hedera helix, English Ivy
Lavandula x *intermedia*, Lavender
Limonium latifolium, Sea Lavender
Miscanthus sinensis, Eulalia or Silver Grass
Oxalis bowiei (formerly *O. bowieana*), Wood Sorrel
Polygonum capitatum, Fleece Flower
Rosmarinus officinalis var. 'Prostrata', Creeping Rosemary
Ruta graveolens, Common Rue
Santolina chamaecyparissus, Lavender Cotton
Tritonia crocata, Tritonia
Vinca major, Creeping Periwinkle
Watsonia species, Watsonia
Zantedeschia aethiopica, Calla Lily

INTRODUCED NATIVE PLANTS

Ceanothus cyaneus, Lakeside Lilac
Ceanothus griseus, Carmel Ceanothus
Dudleya brittonii, Giant Chalk Dudleya
Hesperoyucca whipplei (formerly *Yucca whipplei*), Our Lord's Candle
Romneya coulteri, Matilija Poppy

HISTORICAL TIMELINE

Important people and events
in the history of San Diego Botanic Garden

BEFORE THE LARABEES

1917   Donald Carlton Ingersoll purchases 45 acres in
        Encinitas. He builds a small ranch home on one of
        the parcels, which is 16.5 acres. His wife Gertrude
        ("Nanette" or "Nan,") plants some eucalyptus trees.

1923   Avocado farmer and landholder Anton van Amers-
        foort purchases the 16.5 acres in a foreclosure sale.
        He plants numerous trees, including a grove of
        avocados. The road now called Quail Gardens Drive
        is named Amersfoort Road.

1923   Herman Seidler purchases the 10 acre parcel south of
        the van Amersfoort property from the Union Trust
        Company of San Diego.

THE LARABEE ERA

1926   Ruth graduates from Vassar College and marries
        Charles Larabee. They live in Kansas City, where she
        is a public school teacher, and he is an engineer for
        Larabee Flour.

1931   Charles receives the first half of his inheritance from
        Frederick Larabee's estate. He quits working for
        Larabee Flour and co-owns "The Plant Shop,"
        a nursery in Kansas City.

1936   Charles Larabee receives the second half of his
        inheritance.

1938-42 Charles travels extensively, photographs people and
        landmarks in South America, Mexico, and the
        American Southwest. He participates in an historic
        two-month journey down the Colorado River and

becomes a self-styled expert and lecturer on the American Southwest.

1942   Ruth Larabee purchases a 10 acre parcel from Herman Seidler.

1943   Ruth also purchases a 16.5 acre parcel from Anton van Amersfoort, combining the two properties into a ranch of 26.5 acres. The Larabees move to the ranch from Kansas City. They name it "El Rancho San Ysidro de las Flores" and begin planting trees, shrubs and succulents. Ruth is Troop Leader for Senior Girl Scouts, and Charles is Scout Executive for Senior Explorer Scouts sponsored by the Encinitas Rotary Club.

1944   Ruth Larabee receives her inheritance from Charles Baird's estate.

1946-51 The Lawn House is used as the Scout Hut for Girl Scouts, Explorer Scouts, and Camp Fire Girls.

1949   Charles Larabee establishes a business as a river guide for tours in Utah, Arizona and Colorado. He separates from Ruth.

1950   Ruth and Charles Larabee are divorced. Ruth lives alone on the ranch, and Charles moves to Balboa Island in Newport Beach, California.

1951   Ruth donates 4.2 acres in the southern part of the property to be used by the Boy Scouts. A new "Scout Hut" is built with fund raising and construction organized by the Encinitas Rotary. Charles Larabee marries Lila Pihlblad Hopkins. Ruth becomes the camping sponsor of the Wananka

Camp Fire Girls, headed by Mary Carol Isaacs.

1954   Charles and Lila Larabee move to Shadow Mountain in Palm Desert. Charles continues to participate in and assist the Encinitas Rotary Club.

1955   Ruth offers her property to the San Diego Natural History Museum, but the deal doesn't go through.

1957   Ruth Larabee deeds her property to San Diego County. She leaves for Puebla, Mexico and provides nursing care to needy people at the Baptist mission Hospital Latino-Americana.

1963   Ruth leaves Puebla, Mexico and travels in Europe.

1964   Ruth lives in Lubbock, Texas, and develops a relationship with Texas Tech University.

1968   Charles Larabee dies on February 7 from lung cancer, while living in Palm Desert. Ruth returns to Kansas City.

1969   Ruth Larabee dies on December 26 in a hotel fire in England. In her will and trust she leaves an endowment for the Camp Fire Girls and money to assist nursing students in Mexico. She bequeaths Texas land and funds to purchase a carillon for Texas Tech University in Lubbock. She makes monetary gifts to 70 different friends and family members, and gives money to Tuskegee University in Alabama for scholarships for African American women.

AFTER THE LARABEES LEAVE THE RANCH

1958-60 The County makes room additions to the Larabee House.

1959 The Quail Gardens Foundation By-Laws are adopted July 15.

1960 Gerald Cullison, the Assistant Superintendent of Park Operation and Maintenance for San Diego County, moves with his family into the Larabee House and lives there for two years.

1961 The Quail Gardens Foundation, Inc., is created on March 6. P.J. (Pius John) Miller works at the Garden for San Diego County. He and his wife Chris live in the Lawn House until 1964. After the Larabee House porch is enclosed as an office in 1970, he and his wife move to the Larabee House and live there until his retirement in 1978.

1966 Roads, a parking lot, water lines, bathrooms, and the entrance to the Gardens are installed.

1968 The name of the street on the east side of the Garden is changed from Amersfoort Road to Quail Gardens Drive.

1970 On March 8, Quail Park Botanic Gardens is formally opened to the public. President of the Foundation Julia von Preissig presides over the event.

1971 Paul Ecke, Sr. donates 4.2 acres and the "Scout Hut" to the County for the Garden.

1974 The Scout Hut is remodeled and named the "Ecke Family Building."

1979   The Mildred Macpherson Waterfall opens on March 11, designed and built by Dennis Torzeski and Richard LaFontaine of Torzeski Studios.

1980   The name is changed from "Quail Park Botanic Gardens" to "Quail Botanical Gardens." Gardener Gil Voss is promoted to Horticulturist in and lives with his wife, Alison, in the Larabee House until 1988.

1981   The Docent Society is established by Alison Voss to recruit and train volunteers.

1985   A land swap agreement is made in which property along Saxony Road is traded in exchange for property adjacent to the nursery, with three houses. One of those had belonged to Hans Hartman and his family.

1986   The Visitor Center and Gift Shop open on March 8 and the lower section of the Waterfall stream and pond is completed in the fall.

1992   Both the Overlook Tower and the gazebo in the Lawn Garden are built.

1993   San Diego County tax-funded support operations cease. San Diego County retains title to the land and leases the property to the non-profit Quail Gardens Foundation, Inc., for five years for a nominal amount.

1995   Julian Duval is hired as the first Executive Director (later President and CEO) of the Gardens. The Canary Islands exhibit is installed.

1996   The Bamboo Garden opens. The evening holiday event called Garden of Lights begins.

1997   The Subtropical Fruit Garden is renovated.

1998   The Waterfall area is upgraded and renamed the Tropical Rain Forest.

2000   The Native Plants and Native People display is dedicated to interpret the lifestyle of the Kumeyaay indigenous people who lived in San Diego. A ramada, an ewaa dwelling, a pond, and a stream are constructed. The first Gala fund-raising event is held.

2003   The Seeds of Wonder Children's Garden opens. The City of Encinitas leases the Garden 4.5 acres to the north. The San Dieguito Heritage Museum occupies 1.2 acres.

2004-09 Many of the gardens are renovated with new plantings, and several new gardens are added: The Undersea Succulent Garden, the Mexican Garden, and the South African Garden.

2009   The Hamilton Children's Garden opens, the largest children's garden on the West Coast. The Garden changes its name to "San Diego Botanic Garden."

2012   The Native Plants and Native People Trail is renovated, the Welcome Center admissions building opens, and the Gift Shop (now called The Garden Shops) is renovated.

NAME CHANGES:

1957: Quail Park Botanic Gardens

1970: Quail Botanic Gardens

1980: Quail Botanical Gardens

2009: San Diego Botanic Garden

LARABEE/BAIRD FAMILY TREE

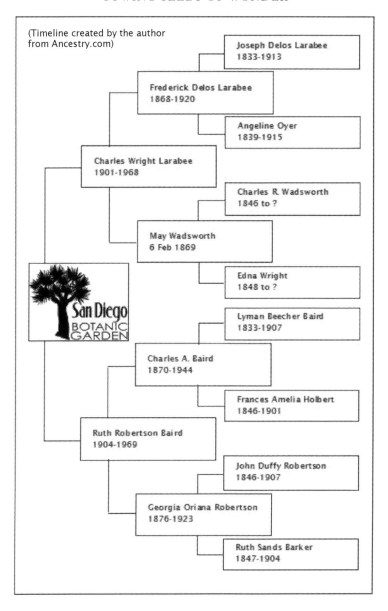

(Timeline created by the author
from Ancestry.com)

Joseph Delos Larabee
1833-1913

Frederick Delos Larabee
1868-1920

Angeline Oyer
1839-1915

Charles Wright Larabee
1901-1968

Charles R. Wadsworth
1846 to ?

May Wadsworth
6 Feb 1869

Edna Wright
1848 to ?

Lyman Beecher Baird
1833-1907

Charles A. Baird
1870-1944

Frances Amelia Holbert
1846-1901

Ruth Robertson Baird
1904-1969

John Duffy Robertson
1846-1907

Georgia Oriana Robertson
1876-1923

Ruth Sands Barker
1847-1904

ABOUT THE AUTHOR

Sally Sandler has been a docent at San Diego Botanic Garden since 2007. She organized volunteer teams that have been instrumental in making the Garden beautiful as well as botanical and has herself tended many of the diverse gardens. Researching the history of the Larabees and other pioneers in San Diego's North County has been her passion for the last five years.

Her work has been published in *Décor and Style Magazine*, *Let's Talk Plants*, the newsletter of the San Diego Horticultural Society, *Quail Tracks*, the newsletter of San Diego Botanic Garden, and the website for the *San Diego Union-Tribune*. She also wrote "Legacy of the Ecke Ranch" on behalf of the Leichtag Foundation. *Sowing Seeds of Wonder* is her first book.

Sandler grew up in the Midwest and attended the University of Michigan, but she has considered herself a Californian since 1972. Her other interests include photography, charcoal drawing, and genealogy. She and her husband share a home in Del Mar, California, and their personal garden was recognized by *San Diego Home and Garden Magazine* recently for its backyard wildlife habitat.

San Diego Botanic Garden has been a place of healing and inspiration for her, and the people there are like an extended family. Her four grandchildren are regulars at the Seeds of Wonder Children's Garden and share the magic with her as often as she can drive them there. Sandler cultivates the flowers outside the Larabee House and can often be found sitting on the wall exactly where Ruth Larabee sat in 1950.

PHOTOGRAPHIC CREDITS

ENDNOTES

[1] "Women's Lifestyles in the 20s and 30s," accessed February 25, 2016, http://classroom.synonym.com/womens-lifestyles-1920s-30s-21530.html.

[2] "Michigan's 'Big Three,' Yost, Baird, Fitzpatrick," *The Newark Daily Advocate*, 1903-10-05, Wikipedia Encyclopedia, accessed September 16, 2010, http://en.wikipedia.org/wiki/Charles_A._Baird.

[3] "Will Become Manager: Michigan Athlete Gets an Unprecedented Offer," *Ft. Wayne News*, 1903-03-21, Wikipedia Encyclopedia, accessed September 16, 2010, http://en.wikipedia.org/wiki/Charles_A._Baird.

[4] Georgia Oriana Robertson was born January 30, 1876 in Jewell, Kansas. 1880 United States Federal Census for Georgie [Georgia] Robertson, [database on-line], Provo, UT, USA: Ancestry.com Operations Inc., 2004, accessed January 19, 2011, http://search.ancestry.com.

[5] Haskett, Wendy, "A Promise Kept to Quail Garden Founder," from "The Backward Glance," column in *North County Times*, July, 1999.

[6] "Transportation History, 1800-1900," from "America on the Move," National Museum of American History, accessed March, 2016, http://amhistory.si.edu/onthemove/themes/story_48_1.html.

[7] *Who's Who in Kansas City*, Who's Who Publishing, Kansas City Public Library, https://local.kclibrary.org/cdm4/item_viewer.php?,"Charles A. Baird," Wikipedia Encyclopedia, accessed 11/19/2010, http://en.wikipedia.org/wiki/Charles_A._Baird.

[8] "Baird Carillon," Wikipedia Encyclopedia, accessed September 16, 2010,

http://en.wikipedia.org/wiki/Charles_A._Baird.

[9] "James Baird (civil engineer)," Wikipedia Encyclopedia, accessed November 1, 2010, http://en.wikipedia.org/wiki/James_Baird_(civil_engineer).

[10] "James Baird State Park," accessed January 20, 2011, http://nysparks.com/parks/101/details.aspx.

[11] "When Freddie Came Marching Home," The Weather-cock, yearbook from Barstow School, Kansas City, Missouri, 1919, pp20-21.

[12] "My Element," The Weather-cock, yearbook from Barstow School, Kansas City, Missouri, 1920, pp17-18.

[13] "Women's Lifestyles in the 20s and 30s," accessed on February 25, 2016, http://classroom.synonym.com/womens-lifestyles-1920s-30s-21530.html.

[14] Author unknown, Stafford County Democrat, 28 January 1886, p1.

[15] Ibid, p2.

[16] Frederick D. Larabee was born June 4, 1868, in Ashford, New York and died April 5, 1920, in Kansas City, Missouri, Ancestry.com, [database online], Provo, UT, USA: Ancestry.com Operations Inc., 2004, accessed March, 2011, http://search.ancestry.com.

[17] Author unknown, "Commander to the Gulf," Time, Time Inc., June 27, 1932, accessed June 2011, http://www.time.com/time/magazine/article/0,9171,743889,00.html#ixz z0zjyD0LXr.

[18] Obituary for Frederick S. Larabee, source unknown, accessed in July 2011, courtesy of the Stafford County Historical and Genealogical Society, 100 So. Main, Stafford, Kansas, 67578.

[19] U.S. Passport Applications, 1795 to 1925, courtesy of Ancestry.com, accessed in August 2011, http://search.ancestry.com.

[20] Newspaper source unknown.

[21] "Mrs. Larabee Gets Half," (name of newspaper unknown,) published sometime c1921.

[22] "Former Hutchinson Man in a Hold-Up," The Hutchinson News, Kansas City, Missouri, December 27, 1923.

23 "Fifteenth Census of the United States: 1930," accessed in 2011, Ancestry.com, http://search.ancestry.com

24 Author unknown, "Couple on 1,800 Mile Water Trip from Kansas City," *Lincoln State Journal*, September 1, 1928, accessed in 2011, Ancestry.com, http://search.ancestry.com.

25 "Fifteenth Census of the United States: 1930," accessed in 2011, Ancestry.com, 2011, http://search.ancestry.com.

26 From the Kansas City Public Library, Missouri Valley Special Collections, Frank Lauder Autochrome Collection, May 1935, accessed in 2011, http://www.kchistory.org/cdm4/item_viewer.php?CISOROOT=/Lauder&CISOPTR=263&CISOBOX=1&REC=19.

27 "U.S. Social Security Act, Application for Account Number," March 31, 1938, accessed in 2011, Ancestry.com, http://search.ancestry.com.

28 Entries from the diaries of Ingaborg Nelani Williamson Midgely, Kansas City, Missouri, 1933 to 1946, courtesy of Nelani Midgely Walker, March, 2016.

29 Barry M. Goldwater, Jr., *Delightful Journey*, Arizona Historical Foundation, Tempe, Arizona, 1940, p1.

30 Norman D. Nevills, "Descent of the Canyons," Region III Quarterly, Vol. 3-No.3, July 1942, p.2, accessed September 2010, http://www.nps.gov/history/history/online_books/region?111/vol3-3i.htm.

31 Nevills, "Descent of the Canyons."

32 Goldwater, *Delightful Journey*. Note that carrier or "homing" pigeons were used as a means of communication for centuries. They were specifically bred for their ability to find their way home over long distances.

33 Melvin, Robert, *Profiles in Flowers: The Story of San Diego County Floriculture*, Paul Ecke Ranch Press, Encinitas, CA, 1989, p59.

34 "Tesoros de Devoción,"New Mexico History Museum, accessed April 24, 2016, http://www.nmhistorymuseum.org/tesoros/tesoros-lightbox/more-text-sats-sy.html.

[35] Deed Book 917, County of San Diego, Office of the Recorder, accessed February 12, 2016.

[36] Popenoe, F.O., "California Avocado Association 1927 Yearbook," 12:41-48, accessed April 10, 2016, http://www.avocadosource.com/CAS Yearbooks/CAS 12 1927/CAS%201927 PG 41-48.pdf, accessed April 10, 2016.

[37] Gerald Cullison, the Assistant Superintendent of Park Operation and Maintenance for San Diego County , Superintendent of Park Operation and Maintenance for San Diego County, in a telephone conversation with the author conducted on December 6, 2010.

[38] Connie (Conrad) Lund, former Girl Scout, in recorded conversation with others who were formerly Scouts with the Larabees, at a luncheon at San Diego Botanic Garden, Encinitas, CA, on March 27, 2012.

[39] Carol (Hasselo) French, former Camp Fire Girl, in recorded conversation with others who were formerly Scouts with the Larabees, at a luncheon at San Diego Botanic Garden, Encinitas, CA, on March 27, 2012.

[40] Haskett, Wendy, "A Promise Kept to Quail Garden Founder," from "Backward Glances," a collection of stories originally published in the column "The Backward Glance," *North County Times*, July, 1999, page unknown.

[41] Caroline Isaacs, in a meeting with the author, Julian Duval and Dave Ehrlinger, at San Diego Botanic Garden, Encinitas, CA, March 18, 2016.

[42] Connie (Conrad) Lund, Ibid.

[43] *The Desert Magazine*, Randall Henderson Publisher, Palm Desert, California, September 1950.

[44] *The Desert Magazine*, Randall Henderson Publisher, Palm Desert, California, April 1949, p37.

[45] Doug Hasselo, former Explorer Boy Scout, in recorded conversation with others who were formerly Scouts with the Larabees, at a luncheon at San Diego Botanic Garden, Encinitas, CA, on March 27, 2012.

[46] Richard Cullum, former Explorer Boy Scout, in recorded conversation with others who were formerly Scouts with the Larabees, at a luncheon at San Diego Botanic Garden, Encinitas, CA, on March 27, 2012.

47 Telephone interview between the author and Julian Duval, President of San Diego Botanic Garden, March 22, 2011.

48 *Ernest Thompson Seton*, from Wikipedia, the free encyclopedia, accessed June 2 2016, https://en.wikipedia.org/wiki/Ernest_Thompson_Seton.

49 Nelson, Kate, "The Ashes of Seton Castle," New Mexico History Museum News Blog, February 2, 2010, accessed June 8, 2016, http://www.nmhistorymuseum.org/blog/?p=185

50 Bob Gooding, Ibid.

51 Caroline Isaacs, in a meeting with the author, Julian Duval and Dave Ehrlinger, at San Diego Botanic Garden, Encinitas, CA, March 18, 2016.

52 Haskett, Wendy, Ibid, p105.

53 Ibid.

54 Behrends, Dorothy S., "Caretaker Outlined for Quail Park, May Become 'Botanical Garden,'" *San Dieguito Citizen*, June 25, 1959.

55 Julian Duval, Ibid.

56 A. Starker Leopold, Sam Blankenship and John Massey, "The California Quail," published by the California Department of Fish and Game, exact date unknown, reported by Don Miller in *Quail Tracks*, February, 1993.

57 Bob Gooding, Ibid.

58 "Balboa Island, Newport Beach," from Wikipedia Encyclopedia, accessed March 22, 2016, https://en.wikipedia.org/wiki/Balboa_Island,_Newport_Beach.

59 William Hopkins, Jr., in an interview with the author and Julian Duval at San Diego Botanic Garden, Encinitas, CA, on December 16, 2010.

60 Ibid.

61 Ibid.

62 Jean Schneider, in a meeting with the author and Julian Duval at San Diego Botanic Garden, Encinitas, CA, March 23, 2016. For more on the history of Jean and Harry Schneider, refer to this link to Harry Schneider's interview conducted in 2012 at the Japanese American National Museum, a

year before he died at age 97.
www.discovernikkei.org/en/interviews/profiles/157.

[63] Bob Gooding, Ibid

[64] Burns, Allison, *Legendary Locals of Encinitas,* San Francisco: Arcadia Publishing, 2012, p30.

[65] *Kansas City Star,* Kansas City, Missouri, June 23, 1953.

[66] Gerald Cullison, Ibid.

[67] There is speculation that the County later dispersed of most of Ruth Larabee's belongings.

[68] Miller, Don, "The Quail Guzzler," *Quail Call,* Vol. 29, No. 1, February 1993.

[69] "Fire Kills 11, Two Americans," *The Vidette Messenger,* Valparaiso, Indiana, December 26, 1969, accessed 2012 through Ancestry.com.

52080525R10143

Made in the USA
San Bernardino, CA
12 August 2017